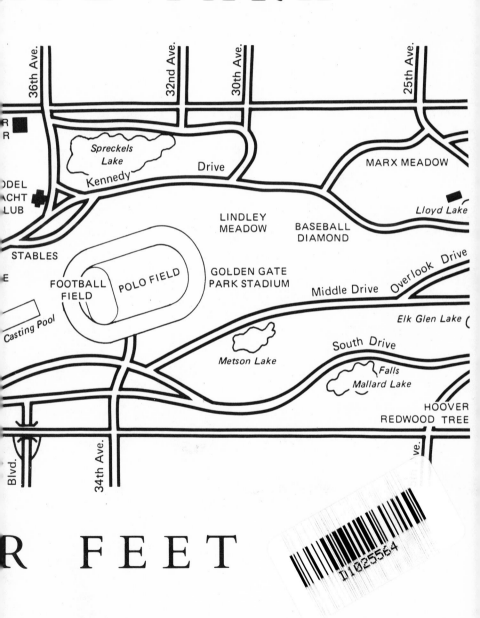

ATE PARK

36th Ave.

32nd Ave.

30th Ave.

25th Ave.

R
R

Spreckels Lake

Kennedy

Drive

MARX MEADOW

ODEL
ACHT
LUB

LINDLEY
MEADOW

BASEBALL
DIAMOND

Lloyd Lake

STABLES

E

FOOTBALL
FIELD

POLO FIELD

GOLDEN GATE
PARK STADIUM

Middle Drive

Overlook Drive

Elk Glen Lake

Casting Pool

South Drive

Falls
Mallard Lake

Metson Lake

HOOVER
REDWOOD TREE

Blvd.

34th Ave.

ve.

R FEET

D1025564

GOLDEN GATE PARK
At Your Feet

Previous books by Margot Patterson Doss

San Francisco at Your Feet
Walks for Children in San Francisco
The Bay Area at Your Feet
Paths of Gold
There, There,
East San Francisco Bay at Your Feet

GOLDEN GATE PARK
At Your Feet

Margot Patterson Doss
with photos by
John Whinham Doss, M.D.

Compiled and Revised from
San Francisco *Chronicle* Series
"San Francisco at Your Feet"

Presidio Press
San Rafael, California
&
London, England

First Edition copyright © 1970 by Margot Patterson Doss

Revised Edition copyright © 1978 by Margot Patterson Doss

First Edition published by Chronicle Books

Revised Edition published by Presidio Press
of San Rafael, California, and London, England,
with editorial offices at 1114 Irwin Street,
San Rafael, California 94901

Library of Congress Cataloging in Publication Data

Doss, Margot Patterson
Golden Gate Park at your feet.

Includes index.
1. San Francisco—Parks—Golden Gate Park.
I. Title.
F869.S37G643   1978   917.94′61′045   78–16678
ISBN0–89141–069–4

All photographs by John Whinham Doss
except for those provided by:
California Academy of Sciences,
pp. 51, 54, 56, 58, 62, 64
De Young Memorial Museum, pp. 72, 75
San Francisco Convention & Visitors' Bureau,
pp. 88, 89, 101, 103
Worden Collection—Wells Fargo History Room,
pp. 114, 153
Art Frisch, pp. 38, 99
Gordon Peters, p. 152

Jacket design by Leslie Fuller

Book design by Hal Lockwood

Printed in the United States of America

"A pedestrian is a creature in fear of its life, but a walker is a man in possession of his own soul."

Contents

Preface

Try to envision a strip of greensward as level as the Marina Green, half a mile wide and stretching from City Hall to the beach. This is what one of the early advocates of Golden Gate Park, a mayor of San Francisco, had in mind for the city. Coincidentally, he was the owner of a grading company and planned to use the leveled excess dirt to fill Mission Bay.

Stretch your imagination even further to people this level corridor with British redcoats marching rank on rank from the seashore to City Hall.

Farfetched? Not as farfetched as one might think. It was the fear of redcoats in the post-Civil War years when Golden Gate Park was emerging that forestalled that level green parade ground. That and the cold northwesterly winds that even today whip down Geary Street.

It was a common belief at the time that parks had to be flat. But thanks to those redcoats that never materialized, and to the prevailing breeze, we have in Golden Gate Park a series of sheltered valleys and natural gentle ridges, baffling to possible soldiers and seawinds alike.

When William Hammond Hall, the designer of Golden Gate Park, submitted his initial plan in 1870, he tipped his hat to Mayor Frank McCoppen with, "It was formerly the practice to make everything assume an artificial appearance, after fixed and regular forms, a seeming attempt to apply the rules of architecture to landscape gardening." Deferentially he continued, "It is therefore with much hesitation that the accompanying plan of a system of roads, walks and other improvements . . . is submitted."

Hall's plan was "to fit a graceful curvature to the natural topography in such manner that the rules of tasteful landscape gardening be combined with the requisites of good engineering principles that much of it might be sheltered from the prevailing northwest winds of summer, while yet taking advantage of the more prominent features from which to produce striking effects in the landscape. . . ."

How sound Hall's plan was, only time could prove. It included three transverse drives that were not built. If they had been, all the many subsequent freeway threats to the park would have been unnecessary.

For the most part, however, Hall's plan has been carried out, including the reclamation of sand dunes. The report of the engineer, "Upon the Management of Sand Downs," with an account of the experiments conducted at Golden Gate Park and "Suggestions for the Prosecution of the Work of Reclamation there Contemplated" is dated 1872.

Within the report one finds descriptions of reclamation of sea downs of Gascony, Denmark, Prussia, Holland, Great Britain, and an outline of the method uniting grasses, lupine, and trees used in San Francisco. In other words, the reclamation project, for which John McLaren is usually given full credit, was actually launched before he came to the park in any capacity. This is not to criticize McLaren, but only to give credit where credit is due.

The first five years of any endeavor are probably the toughest. Land contouring was only the first of many obstacles that lay before Golden Gate Park and its designer. Another was a laborer named D. C. Sullivan. In an almost unbelievable episode, Sullivan, whom Hall had sacked as incompetent, got himself elected to the state legislature. The new legislator went after Hall's scalp with an investigation charging "wanton destruction of trees in Golden Gate Park for firewood for his own use."

Hall was only thinning out "The Forest" in the best of accepted land-management practices, as Federick Law Olmsted and John McLaren, then head gardener of a San Mateo estate, were quick to confirm. The full report of 1876 to the governor of California from the park commissioners of San Francisco discredits the would-be discreditor. It is good for a laugh today. At the time of the new park's beginnings, it must have been a worrisome and time-consuming headache.

Down through the years the friends of Golden Gate Park have far outnumbered the detractors. There was the anonymous clergyman, for example, who smuggled the famous bill creating the park, the Outside Lands Survey "Order 800," up to Sacramento by boat. So violently opposed to the plan for creating a public park system were some of the squatters on what is now park land, they had set a watch on boats going from San Francisco, hoping to waylay the person carrying the bill to the legislature. Who would have thought that it would make its way safely under a clerical habit?

Many of the friends of Golden Gate Park are commemorated in the landmarks there. Stow Lake, named for W. W. Stow, Spreckels Lake, named for Claus Spreckels, Alvord Lakelet, Metson Lake, Lloyd Lake, Murphy Mill, the now departed Sweeney Observatory, and Huntington Falls all fall in this category. So does the M. H. de Young Memorial Museum.

In any definitive history of Golden Gate Park, M. H. de Young will merit a chapter for organizing the California Midwinter International Fair of 1894. The word "midwinter" in the title itself was a stroke of genius for it told an unbelieving world that California could hold a fair while much of the nation was snowed in. To Golden Gate Park it left many legacies, among them the Tea Garden, the Music Concourse, the buffalo and, best of all, the museum.

The stories of John McLaren's long years in the park are too well known to need retelling here. He was a vital force for conservation and a stable figure at a time when stability was growing scarce. There are gardeners alive in the park who knew him well and worked with him and are loyal to him even now. Certainly none of his successors were men of the same measure, with the possible exception of Strybing Arboretum Director Jock (Percy Haddon) Brydon, another uncompromising Scot who developed the arboretum and then returned to private enterprise.

There are hundreds of anecdotes about McLaren, and a score of good ones about Jock Brydon, both colorful men. Much of the hard work of the park is done by men whose self-dramatizing abilities are not so eloquent. I think of testy old Eric Walther, for example, who used to pop out of the hedges the moment one leaned down to smell a flower. Or of Roy Hudson, Jack Spring, Frank Foehr, gardeners all, who rose as executives, Jack to managership.

In its remarkable expanse from the Panhandle to the beach, the park offers something for everyone no matter what his interests. Enjoy it all in its wondrous variety.

Margot Patterson Doss
1970

Introduction
to Revised Edition

San Francisco has such spectacular landscape with its bay, islands, bridges, mountains, and horizons, that walking here is better than any other city in the United States. To live up to this standard takes an equally spectacular park. A great park. And this is what Golden Gate Park is. The only way to really appreciate it is to walk in it.

The classic marathon tour of Golden Gate Park goes from end to end via John F. Kennedy Drive. If you have never done it, consider making this walk your next time out. Like the walk across Golden Gate Bridge, it is something every San Franciscan should do before he dies. It is a four-mile walk if you include the Panhandle, beginning at Baker Street and Oak or Fell streets, and three miles if you begin at Stanyan Street. In either case, pretend for the occasion that you are William Hammond Hall, the landscape engineer who laid out the park, and have returned to see how it is faring more than a hundred years from the time the first trees were planted.

Since it is closed off to traffic at the eastern end on Sundays, use this day and let your route be along what was, until April 2, 1967, Main Drive (now Kennedy Drive). It would have pleased the planner of Golden Gate Park to see the Romanesque park lodge at Fell and Stanyan streets, for his initial plan suggests such a building, although it would undoubtedly shake him a little to find it named for a man he hired as a foreman gardener. Perhaps someday there could be a Hall memorial, too.

The broad lawns through which Kennedy Drive goes characterize this eastern, and first domesticated, end of the park. Hall would expect the next landmark, for it is the oldest and most remarkable building in the park—the Conservatory, presently being considered as an historic landmark. It was Hall who quickly maneuvered a switch of the Conservatory's location from Plateau Mound (renamed Mount Lick), in the northeast corner of the park and thereby safely insured its funding through the legislature.

Early on a museum, a canal, and an aviary were landmarks nearby. In a normal evolution, these have been absorbed elsewhere: the stuffed animals to the M. H. de Young Museum in an earlier phase, the canal and its boats into the function of Stow Lake, and the aviary and its neighboring bear pits into San Francisco Zoo. (When the cherries are in bloom, the walker may want to digress to the Tea Garden at this point via the shortcut behind the de Young.)

On returning to Main Drive, Strawberry Hill would be the next familiar sight to Hall. It stood at this point before the park and became a natural divider for the two halves. From here on to Chain of Lakes, the terrain in Hall's time was all sand dunes; the only other familiar spot would have been the Cliff House.

Today's walkers will find Rainbow Falls, Prayer Book Cross, Crossover Drive (if we had all three of the transverse drives Hall planned, the park could never be overwhelmed by traffic), Lloyd Lake, The Portals of the Past, Spreckels Lake, the Buffalo Paddock, the Dutch windmill, and then the Great Highway. Notice that the ambience changes at Transverse Drive. Cars are permitted, alas, and the quiet, the fresh air, the safety of walkers are all displaced. There is another kind of change—a feeling of wildness, of vast distances, of meadows that might almost be moors when the weather is foggy.

Fair or foggy, it is good walking now, even as it was one hundred years ago. Then it would have been through dunes and experimental grass, perhaps scaring up a wandering cow or un-staked goat. Now it is through swales, on well-paved routes but the mystery of the seaside is still what makes it special.

Margot Patterson Doss
1978

1

Walk the Green Strip

The Panhandle of Golden Gate Park, a quiet island in a noisy swirl of auto traffic, is eight blocks long and one block or 280 feet wide. Newcomers to the city often ask why such an attractive wooded area has such a humorous name, and indeed, the only place this graceful mall looks like the handle of a pan is on a map. The planners of Golden Gate Park didn't intend it to look like the extension of an elongated square skillet, of course.

The boundaries of the park were to have extended along Fulton and Frederick streets as far as Divisadero. Under the law this land was intended for the park, but a singularly tenacious group of squatters had settled in Hayes Valley. To reclaim any land in this area for the park, the city fathers had to compromise and the Panhandle is the result.

To old San Franciscans, the Panhandle is especially dear because it has the most venerable trees in the park. Here in 1871, William Hammond Hall planted the blue gums, Mon-

terey cypresses, and Monterey pines that demonstrated sand
dunes could be converted into park. The credit for taming the
dunes usually goes to "Uncle John" McLaren, but it was Hall
who led the way.

There is a good walk along the Panhandle. It begins at
Baker Street where the Panhandle itself begins, and runs to Stanyan Street. Since May 13, 1903, when President Theodore
Roosevelt scooped out the first shovelful of dirt in the tribal rite
known as "groundbreaking," there has been a monument
named "Justice" at the east end of the Panhandle. It is of
bronze, a female figure about fifteen feet tall by sculptor Robert
I. Aitken, and was placed here as a memorial to President
William McKinley at a time when a whole nation was still re-
coiling from his assassination.

Long ago, in the graceful days of horse and carriage, gently
curving roads led through the plantings of the Panhandle. Since
the automobile is much too dangerous a juggernaut to let loose
among children at play, the old roadbeds have been transformed into grassy meadows. The walker will find that there is a
walkway paralleling both the Oak and the Fell street boundaries
of the Panhandle.

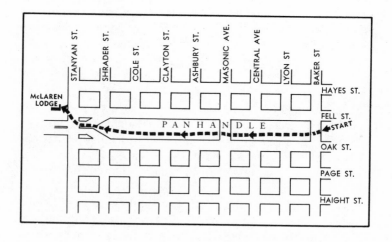

He will also find that the once lush growth of underbrush has been "daylighted," or pruned in such a way that it can be seen through. As the once prosperous bordering communities of the Panhandle had been transformed into the far-out world of the Haight-Ashbury, there had been some street crime here. The "daylighting," which removed hiding places, has successfully reduced this, but it is the better part of prudence not to walk here at night, although rejuvenation is well underway.

By daylight, however, it is as pleasant a walk as any we have (barring the incessant automobile noises). A recently redesigned toddlers' playground at Ashbury on the Oak Street side makes a good halfway stopping place to rest. The Panhandle is a gracious old promenade, one of the few of its kind in the world. It is also a place for chess players, kite fliers, touch football players, and sitters in the sun, whether they be hippie or straight.

2

The Walk McLaren Loved

The San Francisco legend called John McLaren lives on, crusty and larger than life, in the trees he planted, the trafficways he fought, and the sand dunes he tamed in Golden Gate Park. It lives on in the Rhododendron Dell, the building, and the statue memorializing him.

Best of all, the McLaren legend lives on in the gardeners he trained during the fifty-six years he served as superintendent of parks. One of the finest of these is the retired park superintendent, Frank Foehr, who was born in a park, Hamilton Square, April 25, 1906, in a tent in the refugee camp that sprouted after the earthquake and fire.

Like his father, Max, before him, Frank's life has been devoted to gardening, McLaren style, in Golden Gate Park. Not long ago he invited me to duplicate with him a walk McLaren took many times. For the botanist, the history buff, and those who think the east end of the park is too civilized, it is a pleasant and instructive walk indeed.

Begin this walk as "Uncle John" did at McLaren Lodge, Fell and Stanyan streets, a Romanesque building designed by architect E. R. Swain and completed in 1896. McLaren lived here until his death, January 12, 1943, at the age of 96. Colored lights decorating "Uncle John's" Christmas tree, the second to stand on the lawn, are one of the great traditional San Francisco holiday sights. Window boxes filled with flowers also graced every ledge during his lifetime. Then as now, park commissioners' meetings were held in the lodge. The second Thursday afternoon of each month is the regular date for commissioners' meetings and the public, of course, is welcome to sit in. It is worth going in to see the leather-walled commission room with its portrait of John McLaren.

Furniture in the board room has not changed since "Uncle John's" time, but today the living quarters are offices and the department has overflowed into a cleverly concealed addition behind the lodge.

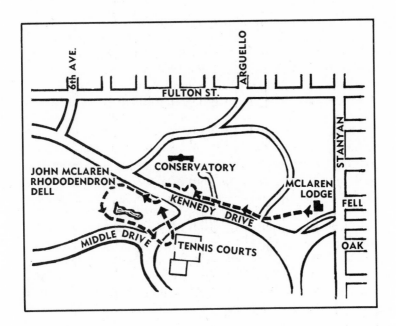

Follow the paved path through the lawn west into the park toward the Conservatory, then parallel to John F. Kennedy Drive. As you walk, look south to spot *The Ballthrower,* by sculptor Douglas Tilden, presented to the park in 1892 by Senator James D. Phelan.

Soon you will be abreast of the Bowles Collection of sweet-smelling Himalayan rhododendrons, given in 1927 by Mrs. Philip E. Bowles in memory of her husband. Earlier the area was called Peacock Valley, for both the peafowl and the ladies who promenaded here.

Beyond the Garfield monument (whose broken sword is intentional), turn right as if to go to the Conservatory. Walk past the everchanging floral plaque and carpet beds to the walkway dead center with the Conservatory. Turn sharp left and follow the tunnel under Kennedy Drive, the safest way in this car-dominated age, to get to the central part of the park.

One emerges in The Rockery, hard by a now-diminished viewing place once called Favorite Point. Turn right, or east, on the paved area. Formerly an equestrian path, it is now especially for cyclists. Follow the asphalt about 100 yards, then leave it for the red-rock path that goes left within the Australian tree fern area, one of the finest anywhere. About parallel to the Arguello Boulevard entrance, bear left again.

The uphill fork in 1890 led to a great wire-covered aviary. Behind it on the hilltop was a wooden bell tower. As Frank Foehr recalls, it called gardeners to work at eight, dismissed them for lunch at noon, summoned them back at one and home at five. The bellringer also fed bears and buffaloes in pits and paddocks nearby. Now the right fork leads through the John McLaren Rhododendron Dell to the Academy of Sciences.

In a few steps downhill on the left, one reaches Quarry Lake, one of many former red-rock quarries in the park. It has also been called the Lily Pond and the Duck Pond. Every five years or so, duckweed takes over and the lake must be drained, dried, and refilled. Frank Foehr, then working during the summer as telephone clerk for John McLaren, recalls the great excitement fifty years ago when sacks of silverware, weapons, and jewelry dumped in the lake by thieves were recovered during the pumping of the lake.

Circle the pond on the south side, past some of the oldest, most gnarled trees in the park. Notice how their roots grasp the extruding Franciscan rocks, a good exposure of radiolaria, oldest fossil in the Bay Area. Soon you will come out on Middle Drive. For quick return, bear left to the tennis courts, then left again through the tunnel under Middle Drive. This tunnel replaced an ornate suspension bridge that stood here in 1894 when a music stand, one of three that have been in the park, and a carriage concourse were located here. The tunnel emerges near Favorite Point, where you can cross Kennedy Drive and return to the Conservatory.

3

Visit the Glass House

The Conservatory in Golden Gate Park looks as though it had been contrived overnight of gossamer and the wings of moths. There is nothing in its mother-of-pearl fragility to suggest circuses, subdivisions, or skyscraper canyons. Yet this, the most durable spun-sugar palace in San Francisco, came 'round the Horn in 1876, is a "big top" of tropical plants and, coincidentally, is a direct lineal, architectural great-grandmother of the prefab unit and the curtain wall.

It is also one of the favorite walks in this city of flower lovers and has been for 100 years. On weekends, sometimes as many as a thousand people an hour stroll the narrow Conservatory aisles to see its "show of shows," changeless and ever changing, like nature herself. The stars are exotic, permanent residents (one dome-filling philodendron is easily fifty years old) and they are enhanced by a chorus of showy blooms chosen for seasonal color and custom. Lilies perform at Easter; cyclamen and azaleas go in January 1, displaying warm reds for Chinese

New Year and Valentine's Day. Around March 16, the spring pastels of cineraria take over the stage in the foyer and the west wing. These are followed in May by the plants children call "pocketbooks," or fishermen's creel, and that gardeners know as calceolaria.

To savor the wedding cake splendor of the building, a purchase from the estate of pioneer James Lick, begin this walk at John F. Kennedy Drive facing the hollow known as Conservatory Valley, a formal promenade set about with carpet beds. One of these floral beds is the most famous sign in San Francisco. This is the announcement plaque, dear to the Convention Bureau, which heralds local civic events in posters of living flowers. Organizations vie for the space a year or more in advance.

To the right of the entrance a plaque notes that the Conser-

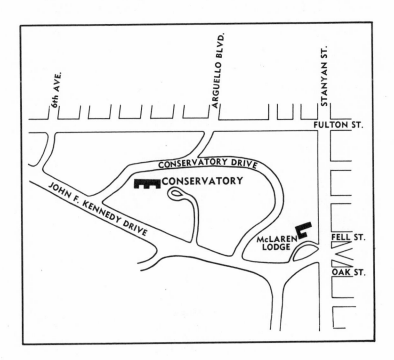

vatory is the "oldest public growing house in California." A much more modest sign at the entrance announces that the public is welcome daily from 8:00 A.M. until 4:45 P.M. There is no charge. Doors that once opened at either end of the building

Conservatory cupolas look like wedding cake ornaments.

have been exchanged for large, clear picture windows above concrete molded to mimic exactly the glass panes set in wood nearby. Vandals and rot impelled the replacements, well worth making since a new Conservatory would cost over several million dollars.

The charming old building, patterned after one at Kew Gardens, was never cheap. Originally it was a gift to the Society of Pioneers. Friends of the park bought it and subscribed the $40,000 cost of putting it up. Lord and Burnham, greenhouse manufacturers, constructed it from prefab panels shipped 'round the Horn from London in 1875. The architect is believed to be Samuel Charles Bugbee, who owes a design debt to Joseph Paxton, creator of the Chatsworth, England, tropical greenhouse in 1837, which had the same kind of dissectable "ridge and furrow" construction. Builders are only now learning that people, like plants, can't take the unobstructed glare through walls of glass.

First-time visitors to the Conservatory are rarely aware of the temperature changes as they walk from room to room, but park gardeners can feel it if it is a degree off. In many rooms the temperatures must undergo seasonal variations but the Pond Room, which drips tropical moisture, is never permitted lower than sixty-nine degrees.

Occasionally, on a weekday morning, the walker used to be surprised to find that the tremendous big palms under the dome seemed fewer. It didn't take a hotel detective to find them. When a large municipal soiree was announced for the City Hall rotunda, the politicians borrowed them. Now palms are lent from the park nursery instead.

4

A Stroll in Rhododendron Row

Rhododendron Dell in Golden Gate Park is one of the great botanical treasures of the world. It is also a place of singular beauty. In May, when the gaudy flowers botanists named in Greek for "rosy fingers" are at their best, no place in the city sings such an unabashed paean to spring. To walk through the warmly sheltered dell, usually silent except for bird song, squirrel chatter, and the soft susurrant leaves, is to step into an enchanted otherworld.

To make this walk, begin at Sixth Avenue and Fulton Street, served by the 5, 16, and 21 Muni buses. Walk into the park, cross John F. Kennedy Drive, and there you are at the graveled mini-court that signals the dell. John McLaren, life-sized and verdigris bronzed as sculptor Earl Cummings saw him, a pine cone in hand, feet planted firmly in the soil, overlooks the whole scene. Some years ago vandals tried unsuccessfully to saw McLaren off his pediment, and it was with some pleasure Assistant Director Tom Molloy pointed out that a friendly fern had grown up to hide the irreparable scar.

Many of the giant "Pink Pearl" rhodies that surround Mc-
Laren are fifty or sixty years old. In 1887, when the great Scot
came to Golden Gate Park, there were only seven varieties of
rhododendron. Soon Sir Joseph Hooker, director of Kew Gardens, sent a fine collection to the park as a thank-you gift to San
Francisco after a visit here. Others were brought to the park
from England in 1912 by John Robert Atkinson, long-time gardener for M. H. de Young. These and the Bowles Collection of
Himalayan rhododendrons were planted on Peacock Lawn, east
of the Conservatory. Now their scions adorn many parts of the
park. The dell as we know it today was started in 1942 with
twelve acres and has expanded as enthusiasm for it grew.

To enjoy its 140 species and infinite varieties, bear right as
you face the statue. Within twenty feet you will be surrounded

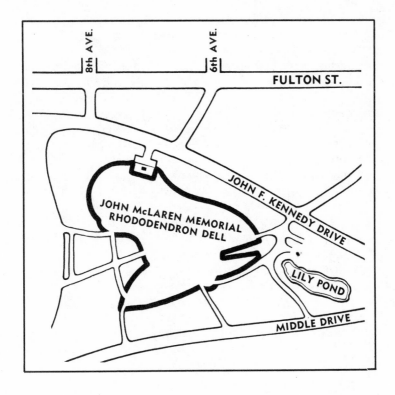

by White Pearl, Mother of Pearl, Cynthia, and Ponticum. Frank Pagliettini, for twenty years gardener to the rhodies, says the latter originated near the Black Sea. It is reputed by the Greeks to have saved them from an invading Persian army who ate wild Ponticum honey, said to be poisonous, as is honey from other rhododendrons.

When you are abreast of a little twenty-foot spruce tree, spring green in new feathery needles, go in to the right to find a sheltered group of flaming red Bulstrode Park, the purply Blue Jay, a bed of wild dutchman's breeches, and blue forget-me-nots in one of the prettiest displays.

Return to the main path and continue right at the first fork, left at the second, and straight ahead at the third to make a circle that will bring you out in the lea of Azalea Hill where Superintendent Emmett O'Donnell estimates there are 263 deciduous azaleas, a small version of the rhododendron, all gleaming on this sunny slope. Shade loving elsewhere, the azalea likes full sun in San Francisco.

At the bench and big cypress, go left and begin another big loop that will reveal dawn redwoods, ferns, and finally a bank of rare yellow rhododendrons. At the two logs, take the low road and thereafter circle right to find the yellow Diane, ruby Garnet, and pink Asthma, which has no connection with the old wheeze of the same name. Fragrantissimum and McNabiae are the white rhodies with the enticing vanillalike odor. Sappho has the purple thumbprint on its virginal corolla. I asked gardener Pagliettini if he talked to the rhodies. "I didn't used to admit it," he said, "but you know, you're out here by yourself working and . . . well I don't babytalk. . . ."

Would he show me?

Well, all right. He walked up to a big red C. P. Rafael and said, as if praising a dancing daughter, "Well, you're making a beautiful show today."

I could almost swear the flowers took a bow.

5

Place for an Old Game

Among the half-remembered sounds of San Francisco yes-
terdays was the merry clang of hand-forged horseshoes against
a steel stake. It was heard behind firehouses, beside livery stables, and near blacksmithies and barns, usually accompanied
by a sandy ka-thunk, and the happy shouts of players and yard-
birds.

Paul Revere may have played horseshoes long before he
took his midnight ride, for the game was a popular American
pastime in colonial days. For that matter, Hercules too may
have pitched a few when he rested from his labor of cleaning
the Augean stables, for the game, as quoits, using a complete
ring rather than the lucky open-ended loop we know, has been
traced to the ancient Greeks.

Unlike the rhythmical creaking of buggy harness and the
song of the tonga bar, horseshoe ringers are a nostalgic sound
that can be recaptured in San Francisco almost any fair afternoon with a walk round the recently brushed-out northeast
corner of Golden Gate Park.

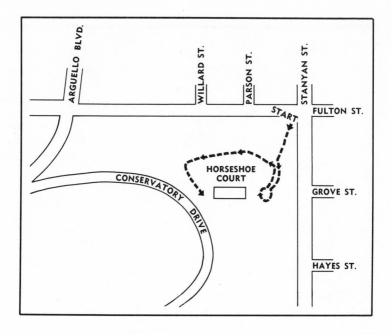

Begin this exploration at the Fulton-Stanyan street corner of the park, bearing left uphill on a red-rock path. The original topographic survey map of the park shows a hill at the terminus of Grove Street at 384 feet, the second highest point in the park and topped only by Strawberry Hill. In 1870, William Hammond Hall conceived this elevation as a viewpoint, which he named Plateau Hill, and which he considered an ideal site for a conservatory.

It lost its name in a neat legislative maneuver on September 7, 1874, according to Guy and Helen Griffen in *The Story of Golden Gate Park,* when the park commission renamed the hill Mount Lick to confuse a "Sand-lotter" in the State Legislature who was objecting to appropriating money for erecting a conservatory. As his opening argument, the politico attacked the choice of a site. Before he could proceed, he was asked to show on the park map the exact site he opposed. The site, of course, had been shifted in the renaming and wasn't on the map. The appropriation passed while the fellow sat down, trying to look as though he didn't have egg on his face.

As you walk around the crest, if you can take your eyes from the unexpected vistas this slight elevation reveals now that the tangled underbrush is gone, notice the free-form concrete ledge that extrudes occasionally through the earth underfoot.

A reservoir holding 100,000 gallons of water and containing a garden of aquatic plants once adorned this space. The water was used to irrigate Panhandle and park grounds below. Early on, a park nursery stood where McLaren Lodge, the red-tiled roof barely visible through the trees below, now stands. Long-time gardeners like former Superintendent Frank Foehr still refer to the area here as Old Reservoir Hill.

To track down the clang of the horseshoes echoing through the trees, look through the fence on the western side of the crest, then retrace your steps to the asphalt path. Follow it southwesterly until it forks. (This will be beyond the locked stone comfort station in the live oak thicket uphill.)

This monumental horse was created in bas-relief in 1937.

Take the left fork of the path around a wooded curve and up the stone steps. Suddenly—pow!—there in the cliff on whose apex you stood a few moments ago is a tremendous dappled gray horse, a primitive pop-art bas-relief in concrete, set off by a stunning yellow acacia tree.

Old-timers playing in the horseshoe pits under it will tell you it was created in 1937 by one of their number, Jesse S. (Vet.) Anderson. Another bas-relief by Anderson, of a horseshoe player encircled by a shoe, is near the area clubhouse.

In the oral history of the San Francisco Golden Gate Horseshoe Club is the persistent memory that this area was a quarry before the Works Progress Administration created the elegant stone work. Sure enough, early park reports document that red rock for roads was once quarried here.

Live oaks on the hills above have watched both work crews and horseshoe pitchers lo, these many years, for this area, too, was part of "The Forest," the indigenous flora that park planner William Hammond Hall thriftily employed. If you'd like to try your hand at horseshoes (or need a key to the comfort station), ask at the clubhouse.

6

A Bright Corner

One of the persistent misconceptions about Golden Gate Park is that originally it was all sand dunes.

Not so. A quick look at the First Biennial Report of the San Francisco Park Commissioners, covering the years 1870–71 and printed by the quaintly named Francis & Valentine, Steam Book and Job Printers, dispatches that delusion in a hurry.

"The Golden Gate Park contains about 1000 acres, of which 270 acres at the eastern end is good arable land, covered in many places with trees and shrubbery; this portion may at once be converted into an attractive resort," wrote William Hammond Hall, surveyor, planner and first superintendent of the park. "The remaining 730 acres stretching down to the ocean beach, is a waste of drifting sand. Forbidding as it appears at present, it is confidently believed that it can be reclaimed by proper appliances."

Hall went on to describe the indigenous flora. "Of the arable portion of the Reserve, the northern slopes and tops of the ridges and hills are, as a general thing, covered with a dense growth of scrubby Live Oak *(Quercus agrifolia)* and California Lilac *(Ceanothus thysiflorus)* of a maximum height of 14 or 18 feet, interspersed by a few Red Berried Elders of nearly equal height and here and there a stunted specimen of the California Cherry . . ." Under the oaks, he reported, was dark sandy loam covered with six to ten inches of leaf mold.

The old ceanothus are gone, but many of the native live oaks, which grew from the roots of trees cut over before the park was acquired and again after the 1906 earthquake, are still to be found in "The Forest" at the northeast corner of the park within the area confined by Arguello, Fulton, and Stanyan streets and the park's North Ridge Drive (also called Conservatory Drive on some maps).

Walkers who explore this earliest developed area of the park will also find that it has been newly perked up after thirty years of desultory maintenance.

Begin this walk at the Arguello Boulevard gate on Fulton. The bus stop cobbles and plantings are new, but the pointed stone wall has been there since 1901. The imposing pair of ornamental pillars was erected in 1915 by Philomen Clarke to commemorate Crawford E. Clarke, and looked, in those days, like a monumental spillover from the cemetery that stood just uphill to the northeast on Lone Mountain.

Go into the park and start uphill immediately on your left on some new railroad-tie steps. Notice how nicely they have been mortised in to preserve existing tree roots. Walk east on a neatly curried red-rock path, parallel to Fulton Street. The path meanders through wooded thickets of live oaks, gnarled and contorted as a sea of stationary serpents. A pause on one of the view benches reveals glimpses of the Golden Gate Bridge towers, the Pacific Ocean and Mount Tamalpais. Continue east until you reach the short, straight Willard Street asphalt path. In 1872, it was a carriage road. Cross it and continue on the tie steps uphill.

Within a few steps, just beyond the fat-trunked ostrichlike tree, you will reach a glade. The mulch underfoot is made up of

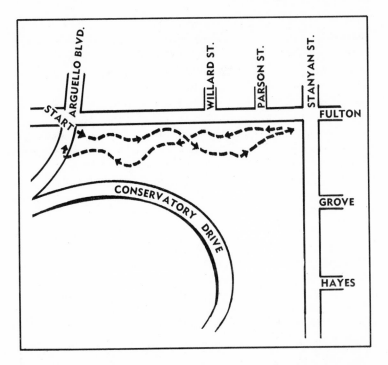

wood chips from a brush-chipping machine. The fallen limbs and other debris that formerly made this corner of the park a vine-tangled jungle have been returned to the soil, speeding Mother Nature's thrifty reclamation of vegetable matter and saving the taxpayer hundreds of dollars once spent on trash hauling.

Some equally thrifty play equipment, designed by Beckwith and Langsner and using salvaged "organic materials," has been installed. A talk tube, sandboxes made of huge excavator tires, a climber of fir beams, swings that use tree trunks, a free-form tunnel are among the toys.

Pick up the asphalt path and head northeast on it to reach the Stanyan-Fulton corner, where tables, just the right size for cards, chess, or novel writing, have been placed in the sun.

To return to Arguello gate, take the red-rock path that crisscrosses the route you travelled. It loops along the park about twenty feet higher on the transverse ridge of Franciscan shale you have been walking. The large bare circle you pass was once the site of a rustic pavilion for picnickers. As you walk, try to imagine ladies in leg-of-mutton sleeves, sweeping skirts, and wide-brimmed leghorn straw boaters as they promenaded here in the Gay Nineties, enjoying San Francisco's "new" park.

7

Three Gardens in the Park

Nostalgia takes some interesting turns along the path of days. Currently one of them is enthusiasm for plants. Simultaneously there is a resurgence of the ferny indoor plant craze of Victorian days and a mania for exotica reminiscent of the forties. The Conservatory is a showplace of the former. Near it, the Fuchsia Garden, the Dahlia Garden and the older cactusy Arizona Garden are strongholds of the latter. We may not think of fuchsias, dahlias, and agaves as exotic in San Francisco because they grow so well here, but half the world certainly does.

Both the Fuchsia and Dahlia gardens are at their best in August. To enjoy a walk through them, begin at Fell and Stanyan streets (handy to the 21 Hayes municipal bus line). Walk up the semicircle of driveway that approaches McLaren Lodge. Just beyond the main entrance to the lodge, look for an asphalt walkway that brings one past the big swamp cypress tree, a native of the Everglades that turns brown in winter. In August it is a lush green.

When the path curves out to parallel John F. Kennedy Drive, follow it west, across Conservatory Drive, then take the next paved walk that takes off to the right. This will bring you alongside Peacock Lawn, where in the Gay Nineties peacocks used to preen before a mirror. Some of them were human. Just past the brilliant orange bed of montbretias, swing off to the right. Soon you will be abreast of three young macadamia trees and a young redwood, all recently planted. When you reach a bed of red Scarletta begonia, backed by blue forget-me-nots, planted to point up the gray of a deodar, begin to look for the Fuchsia Garden just beyond, As tempting as it will be to take the fork that goes down into the valley, forebear. Instead take the hard left uphill path. Fanfare, a fuchsia hybridized by the Victor Reiters, senior and junior, during the fuchsiamania of the late 1930s, is the first of these lovely flowers one meets.

As you walk along the high path, look downhill to see a fantasy costumed and choreographed by Mother Nature. There are standard fuchsias whose ballerina-like flowers cascade out in shooting-star formations. There are vining types whose flowers explode like fireworks from a tree above. There are hedges

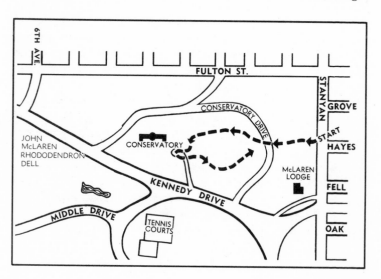

of dainty fuchsias, marching along primly, and tree fuchsias that look like lilacs until one is close enough to see that each bloom is a miniature of the prima ballerina.

When you pass through the memorial grove of redwood trees, each commemorating a loved one gone, begin to look underfoot for white splashes. A great horned owl has taken up residence in the eucalyptus just beyond. Look up and you may catch a glimpse of him in the tallest tree. Take the middle path on the right at the next junction, and twenty steps beyond, bear left to reach the Dahlia Garden, displaying our City flower. Many have great shaggy hippy heads. Others are shorn neatly as civil servants.

Go up the steps beyond to reach the Conservatory. Explore the Conservatory if you have not yet done so, then retrace your steps to the top of the staircase, bear left for thirty feet, then right. This brings you to "The Gallery" of the 1894 Arizona Garden. By bearing around to the right, then left uphill, you will reach two view spots, much favored by oldsters, squirrel feeders, pigeon fanciers, and sun worshippers. From the upper one, go east on Conservatory Drive about ten feet, then right, downhill to seeing into the Fuchsia Garden beyond a grove of native oak trees. Bear left at the next cross path, and left again at the following one. When Barney Barrons, supervisor of this section, took me along this way, we found an old gentleman and his wife feeding three jays, six squirrels, and several overfed pigeons at the benches here, like a vignette from the *Peaceable Kingdom*, until a dog arrived, homing in on the birds. The red-trunked tree on your left is the syncarpia of Australia, known there as "the turpentine tree."

When you have passed through the center of the Fuchsia Garden, the path rejoins Conservatory Drive. Cross it and walk through the little meadow. Half a block takes you out at Hayes and Stanyan streets, handy to public transportation again.

8

"Big Rec," A Sporting Walk

The summer game American boys love beyond all else has long been baseball. In Golden Gate Park, the classic place to see it is "Big Rec," as generations of kids have nicknamed the big recreation green first laid out by William Hammond Hall in the original park plan of 1870.

As any boy who grew up "out in the avenues" can tell you, a quick and easy way to get there is via the walk that enters the park at Fifth Avenue and Lincoln Way. About one short block brings the walker to South Drive. Cross it and there going into shrubbery is a macadam walk with the stenciled message in white No Bicycles. Go in. Within a few steps the walk curves into the east end of the grassy meadow where three baseball or softball games are sometimes in progress simultaneously.

As you walk, notice on your right, well hidden in the trees, the park nursery. In 1924 when Kezar Stadium bumped it from an earlier location at Stanyan and Beulah streets, the nursery usurped about half the acreage initially devoted to the green. At

26

one time nine ball diamonds were comfortably located on this area. For a while recreation directors tried to continue scheduling the nine diamonds in condensed space with small portable screens. In those days kids called the field "Big Wreck," and, according to one veteran observer, "The games were so close together then, it's a wonder someone wasn't killed."

Follow the curving walk and soon you are approaching a blocky building that houses the handball courts. If the door is

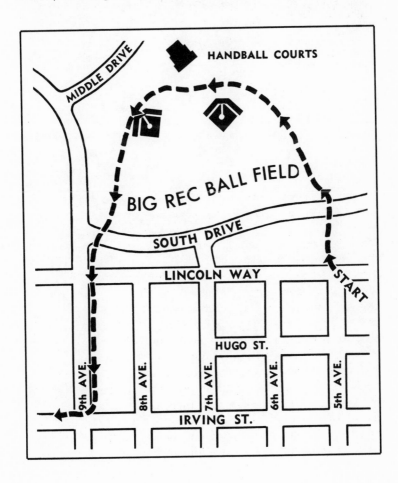

open, go in to find a small glassed-in gallery that often reveals the game in progress below. Steps outside lead not to a higher gallery but to a furnace room whose heater keeps the cement walls from sweating, a hazard in handball.

Nine baseball diamonds were planned by William Hammond Hall for this area.

Continue along the walk as it swings behind Nealon Grandstand, named for James J. Nealon, originator of the benefit fund for injured ballplayers. Its neighbor, Graham Grandstand, commemorates Charles Graham, first owner of the San Francisco Seals. Men from industrial and semipro leagues usually play here on Sundays. The boys in youth recreation leagues are more apt to be on the fields during the weekdays and at twilight times.

Look north, over the green of dividing trees, for a glimpse of Morrison Planetarium, about half a block north of the grandstands. The walkway between the refreshment stand and handball courts would bring you out near it on Middle Drive. For this walk, however, curve behind the grandstands and make a semicircle around the field.

During the California Midwinter International Exposition of 1894, an earlier grandstand stood here overlooking an athletic grounds and racetrack. Also on the field at the western end was a festival hall, a round racing-horse pavilion, the San Mateo County Exposition Building, a replica of its county courthouse, a restaurant, and a forest of automotive windmills.

Soon the walk curves gently toward Strybing Arboretum, then straightens out, pointed toward Ninth Avenue. You will emerge on Lincoln Way a few blocks west of your starting place.

9

Kezar Stadium

The least parklike part of Golden Gate Park is the concrete corner bounded by Stanyan, Waller, Frederick streets and Arguello Boulevard. So ugly is it, indeed, that at least one excellent guide book, *Buildings of the Bay Area,* by John and Sally Woodbridge, has ignored it. These astute critics cavalierly nipped this blip of land right out of their park map on the reasonable contention that buildings do not a garden make, nor parking lots a park.

The land is part of the Golden Gate Park acreage, however. Mundane as the grounds have become since 1925 when Kezar Stadium was built on the site of the park nursery and some acquired railroad lots, it is still a mecca for baseball, football, basketball, soccer, and track fans.

A walk around it is to do once, in the spirit of exploration. Thereafter, no one walks here for pleasure, except as a shortcut into Children's Playground, or *en passage* to a game.

To make this walk, begin at Waller Street and Stanyan. At the outset, look west along Waller to locate Park Station of the San Francisco Police Department hidden in the trees. It was here that John McLaren's men once shoveled away the concrete poured for paving as fast as the city works department dumped it. He prevailed then, but he must be spinning in his grave to see what has happened nearby. By reputation the kindest cops in the city are the Golden Gate Park mounted police. Their stables and office are near Angler's Lodge and the polo field parallel to Thirty-sixth Avenue.

Walk south on Stanyan Street and the next building is a basketball pavilion, which seats 5,500. High school and college teams often play here. Go a few more yards south and brace yourself for the dreariest parking lot north of Los Angeles. This area could logically sustain demonstration plantings on parking-lot concealment. It does not. Trees and tennis courts stood here while McLaren was alive.

Look west. There, looming overhead, is the Mary A. Kezar Memorial Stadium, an impregnable fortress whose main entrance is puzzling to find. Erected in 1924 with the $100,000 Kezar bequest plus $200,000 appropriated by the city, both pavilion and stadium were designed by Willis Polk & Co., in association with Geoffrey Bangs, Thomas F. Chase, C. F. Masten, and Lester W. Hurd. Fans of Willis Polk prefer to forget that he had anything to do with it. The only place where the romantic niceties of the Willis Polk style are evident are on two memorial benches within, one to Mrs. Kezar and her brothers Bartlett, Charles, and John Doe. (Yes, Virginia, there was a John Doe.) The other bench commemorates Tony Morabito, founder of the Forty-niners, the pioneer major league professional football team on the Pacific Coast. When the building opened with a track meet, May 2, 1925, Paavo Nurmi, the Finnish marathon champion, was the featured attraction and the building was only half as high. Capacity crowds at the Army-Navy games inspired the recreation staff to double the size of the stadium. It now seats 60,000. The press box is the turret sticking up on the

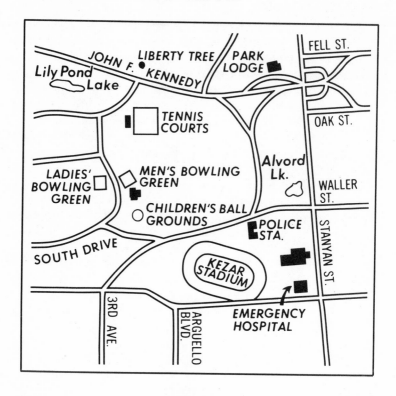

south rim. A veteran's shelter, which can accommodate twenty-six wheelchairs and is served by an elevator, looks over the north rim. Those six floodlight towers are eighty feet high.

Continue on Stanyan Street and the next structure is Park Emergency Hospital, part of the city's public health network. It nosed into the park at a location on the Music Concourse during the Midwinter Fair of 1894, staffed with twelve physicians and volunteer nurses from St. Luke's and Children's hospitals. Like the police station, it now serves the surrounding residential community, and since it is really extraneous to the park, should better have been located out among the houses and shops.

If by now you have had your fill of concrete, turn back on

Stanyan and retrace your steps. At Haight Street there is an entrance that leads within a few steps to Alvord Lakelet, and beyond that, a tunnel that soon brings you out into grass and lawns. Who wants to walk amid bumpers, headlights, and concrete where no birds sing?

10

A Peaceful Dell

Golden Gate Park has many half-remembered secrets. One of them is De Laveaga Dell, a natural, narrow green-tented glen whose special enchantment seems to be a kind of quiet happiness. It is as though some *genius loci* long ago had said, "Let this ever after be a merry place" and ever after, it was. This genie of place could well have been Monarch, the great grizzly bear who once inhabited bear pits at the western end.

To reach De Laveaga Dell by the most scenic route, begin at the Conservatory. Walk out the front door dead ahead through Conservatory Valley and through the tunnel under John F. Kennedy Drive. It will bring you out at Favorite Point. Cross the bicycle trail and bear left through The Rockery. Inside of 100 yards you will be in a second tunnel, this one under Middle Drive, which gives on the tennis courts. At the clubhouse, turn right, cross Bowling Green Drive behind it and lo, there is a walk sloping down through rhododendrons into De Laveaga Dell.

As you reach the lowest level, look to the left at the little meadow. Originally this was designed as a small lake. In rainy season, a little *playa* lake or sump still develops here. (There is only one sewer in the entire park.) As it does in wilderness, in many low parts of the park ground water seeps down to the water table. In the city, the water table is continually dropping and in another few years the little lake in De Laveaga Dell will be only a memory. Feeding it in the spring presently, however, there is often a charming four-inch-wide rivulet at the eastern end, surrounded by native grasses, mimicking a larger stream, like a gem of *bonseki* or miniature tray landscape.

The main attraction in De Laveaga Dell is a natural creek, singing in springtime and dry in summers, like a little bit of Marin County transplanted. Keep walking west and soon you will reach it, just beyond two gigantic elms. Just past the large bed of St. John's wort, look uphill on the north bank for a large dedication stone, acknowledging the philanthropy of Joseph V. de Laveaga, who made this improvement possible. The de Laveagas were once owners of a third of *Rancho Quien Sabe* in San Benito County and the court case that followed the death of Maria C. de Laveaga in Spain in 1904 is a California probate classic. A dotty aunt and a deathbed marriage are but two of its titillating facets.

As natural as the dell looks, its rocks and stream were the contrivance of John McLaren, who used the pre-existing canyon as his inspiration. In 1902, the year the dell was improved, the report of the park commissioners says, "This recent improvement occupies the site of what was known as the Deer Glen, the deer having been moved south across the drive to a new enclosure. This lovely spot, abounding in every natural beauty, lies between two high sloping banks, along which a footpath has been laid leading to the west and where overhanging oaks form a leafy canopy, revealing from the eastern end of this little dell an interior worthy of the brush of any painter. In this interior is formed a creek bed, flanked by large boulders where the tiny stream meanders over a pebbly bottom in an irregular course to a small sheet of water below. On the sides are outcroppings and ledges of rocks, in whose pockets and crevices grow cotyledons, ferns, echeverias and mosses. . . ."

Today the native plants are threatened by biddy-biddy, a ground-covering pest from New Zealand that has invaded the dell. Six iris beds, each about sixty feet long and thirty feet wide, once filled the area east of the lake. One long-time park buff can remember botanizing through De Laveaga Dell with her father, when every tree was tagged with its Latin name— "As children we learned the names of trees in Golden Gate Park that way."

Climb uphill at the western end of the dell to reach the meadow where Monarch's bear pit was located. The gift of William Randolph Hearst, Monarch launched the park

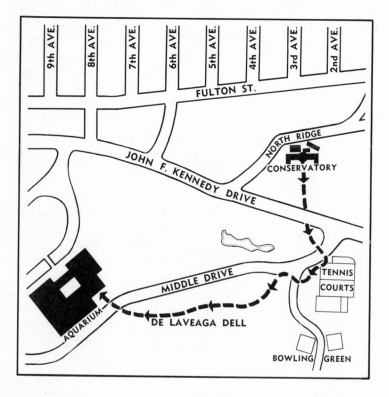

menagerie, which ultimately became San Francisco Zoo. To see him, stuffed, cross the harlequin paving of Middle Drive and go into the Academy of Sciences by the back door. He is sometimes on display in the new foyer of the academy.

If a set of tennis or game of lawn bowling is more your speed, circle back on the path that borders the dell's southern floor. It terminates at Bowling Green Drive, west of the tennis courts, north of the bowling greens.

11

A Walk in the Bard's Garden

What is in the mysterious locked green box in the garden behind the Academy of Sciences?

As the Bard of Stratford-upon-Avon said, at least four times, "Thereby hangs a tale." I will not reveal it straight away "Lest too light winning make the prize light."

If you would truly learn with your own eyes, come to the Garden of Shakespeare's Flowers, commonly miscalled the "Shakespeare Garden," on South Drive in Golden Gate Park. The puzzling metal box can be opened on request to the park office.

Begin this scholar's walk across from Strybing Arboretum between Middle Drive and the Music Concourse where a sign saying Shakespeare Garden indicates a macadam walkway. Follow the walk northeast about half a block. There will be a hill on your left, a waist-high hedgerow of English laurel on the right. Look for a gap midway in the hedgerow. The stone underfoot announces quietly, "The Garden of Shakespeare's Flowers established by the California Spring Blossom and Wildflower Association in 1928."

Go in through the gap, walk about fifty feet toward the left to find a chart of the garden and a numbered identifier of twenty plants featured in the works of Shakespeare. This is but a fraction of the flowers mentioned by the Bard. Between aconitum, aloes, and wormwood and yew are some 150 more, among them such exotics as bilberry, eglantine, gillyvors, lady smocks, lark's heels, mandragora, osiers, and samphire.

"When daisies pied and violets blue and lady smocks all silver white and cuckoo buds of yellow hue do paint the meadows with delight. . . ."

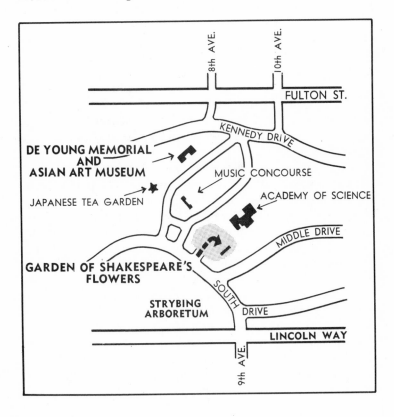

To check out this quote, and dozens more, walk to the deepest border of the garden where floral quotations on six bronze panels, each purchased by a different city group known for cultural interests, flank the green box. The Bohemian Club, the San Francisco Garden Club, the English-Speaking Union, the American Association of University Women, the Creative Writers of California and the P.E.N. Club were the generous donors. The contents of the green box, however, came to San Francisco as a gift from the town of Stratford and its former mayor, Archibald Flower, a name that might have been coined by the Bard along with Dame Quickly, Bottom, Simple, Shallow, Nym, or Pistol.

If you haven't guessed by now, within that vaulted box is a likeness of the poet whose allusions made possible this leafy bower.

As it happens, it is one of two copies of the bust cast in bronze by George Bullock in 1914 from a carving hewn of soft stone by Garrett Jansen before 1623. The other copy stands on the north wall of Holy Trinity church in Stratford-upon-Avon. For Shakespearean scholars, it is the familiar bust holding the quill pen upon a pillow mentioned by Leonard Digges in the *First Folio*.

It is believed to have been modeled from either a life or death mask, to have been commissioned by the poet's son-in-law, Dr. John Hall, and to have had the approval of Mrs. Shakespeare. The *Encyclopedia Britannica* gives half a column to descriptions and whether or not the nose was broken and subsequently repaired.

Well might that mysterious green box be locked against vandals. This is truly a treasure.

When you have tarried here awhile, find the Alice Eastwood Bench honoring the long-time director of botany for the Academy of Sciences. This garden was Dr. Eastwood's idea. Appropriately, her bench is such a place as might suit that sailor's wife mentioned in Macbeth, who had "chestnuts in her lap and munched and munched and munched." Or where Othello might murmur, "not poppy nor mandragora, nor all the drowsy syrups of the world shall ever medicine thee to that sweet sleep."

When time hangs heavy, look for the sundial that counts only the sunny hours. Then slip through the hedge nearby to find behind a great magnolia a leviathan's bones. Never heard of a leviathan? To paraphrase the man whose writings have influenced the English language more than any source except the Bible—a leviathan by any other name might be a whale.

12

Historic Tree Lane

Half-forgotten, almost eclipsed by grander, if sometimes ir-relevant, projects, is San Francisco's own tribute to the founding of our nation, 1776 and all that. It is an historic double lane of trees planted in 1896, twenty years late for the U.S. Centennial, eighty years early for the U.S. Bicentennial. No matter. Each tree was selected from a place Destiny fingered in the original states of the Union. The cedar, for starters, came from Valley Forge. Another tree is from the grave of Thomas Jefferson. Along with the trees, of course, came more than a handful of the soil of each momentous place to mingle inspirationally with the soil of San Francisco.

The Historic Tree Grove, as it is known, stands just off John F. Kennedy Drive near the Pioneer Log Cabin.

To make this walk, transport yourself to Fulton Street at Park Presidio Drive. Go into the park on the walk on the south side of Park Presidio and continue past the Rose Garden. Take the next path (before traffic, the continuation of Fifteenth

Avenue). This will lead you through the Native Sons and Daughters Redwood Memorial Grove, a group of thirty-seven redwoods commemorating heroes who fell in World War I, as Earl Cummings' bronze statue *The Doughboy* attests. The boulder near the path entrance gives the names of the fallen.

Cross Kennedy Drive and look for the double row of trees several hundred feet left of Stow Lake Drive. Pioneer Log Cabin, a replica of an early settler's home built in 1911 as a meeting hall for the Association of Pioneer Women, will be off to the right beyond a spacious lawn. Enter the lane and be prepared for a surprise. Only half a block long, it seems to have its own enchantment. Like the nation it salutes, there is no end in sight. Planted by the Sequoia Chapter, Daughters of the American Revolution, to commemorate the surrender of Cornwallis at Yorktown, 1785, its story is modestly told on a boulder near the far end, placed here in 1920. When you have enjoyed its East Coast ambience, leave the lane and walk toward Pioneer Log Cabin to look for three other memorial trees, one planted in 1903 by the Native Daughters of the Golden West and the two oaks near it planted by the San Francisco Garden Club in 1927 in memory of Willis Polk, San Francisco architect known for his love of trees.

When you have discovered them all (and found the hand-hewn chair made from a stump) pass the Pioneer Log Cabin and head for the path that circles Stow Lake. Bear left on it, away from the refreshment stand, and continue past the Roman Bridge, following Stow Lake Drive until you are standing at its sharp turning point. Pause here a moment to look up at what was once Huntington Falls, one of the most attractive ornaments to the park. In the park's master plan, this waterfall, and the creek represented by the point of water between your toes and Strawberry Hill, continue on into the Japanese Tea Garden. To follow its course, cross Stow Lake Drive and take either of the two walks that slope downhill here. At the point where they join, notice the boulders grasped by the tree roots. Those white quartz veins represent the cascading water in Japanese symbolism. So do the stairs. Continue down them and in a few

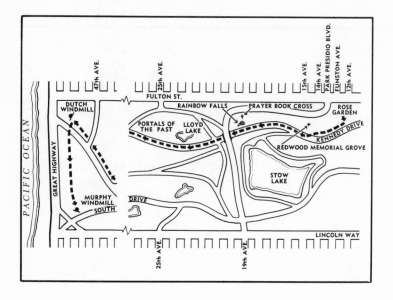

yards you are at the gate to the Tea Garden. Bear right, and go into the first open gate. The stream continues here.

Of course, if American colonial, rather than Spanish colonial history is your choice of tea party, you can always wend your way back toward the far end of the Music Concourse where the Francis Scott Key statue has been re-erected, where he can balance the Bandshell in appropriate Beaux Arts formality. Then return to Kennedy Drive and bear east toward the Conservatory where the southwest corner holds the handsome sequoia known as "The Liberty Tree," planted in 1894 on the anniversary of the Battle of Lexington.

13

Children's Playground

A great Christmas present was given to the young and young in heart of San Francisco in December 1977. The construction fences came down at the redesigned Children's Playground and the result looked as if it just came out of Santa's workshop.

San Francisco doesn't make much of its "firsts," but this one was the great-great-granddaddy of a million public playgrounds. Also known as "The Children's Quarters" and as "Sharon Playground," when it was completed in Golden Gate Park in 1887 with a generous bequest from Senator William Sharon, it became the first children's playground to be established in a public park in America. There was one private playground in the East, but that was it. Today every self-respecting city, town, village, school, subdivision, and shopping center boasts a playground or kiddie lot. Now renamed the Mary E. Connally Playground, in honor of a much loved former park commission secretary, it is well worth a pilgrimage of exploration, however, for the grandsire had something many of

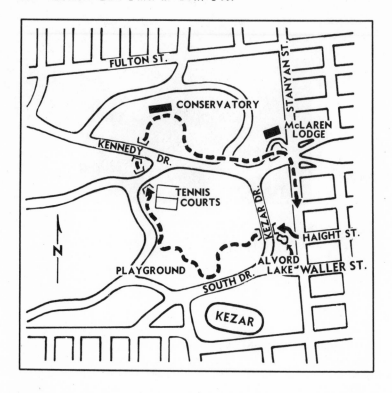

the descendants lack—style, grace, and space. For those who are equally interested in adult play, this walk has an added inducement: Nearby are the lawn bowling greens and "The House that Jack Built." Stroll along Bowling Green Drive to the tennis courts and there are two great shortcut underpasses that will bring you out at the Conservatory. A few more strides down John F. Kennedy Drive can take you past "Uncle John McLaren's Christmas Tree" in front of the park lodge.

To make this loop walk, begin at Haight and Stanyan streets, surely one of the easiest places in the city to reach by public transportation. It is served by Muni buses 7, 33, 71, and 72. Following the route that William Hammond Hall planned so children could reach Children's Playground safely without crossing streets, walk into the park at Haight Street, heading for Alvord Lakelet, a gift from William Alvord, an early park commissioner. Circle the lake on either side to find on the far end an underpass, a cavelike, pre-stressed concrete bridge studded with stalactites. It is also a prototype. Appreciative engineers installed the plaque at the approach a few years ago.

Kezar Drive, which has been reduced to a commuter's chute in recent years, thunders overhead, barely noticed from this safe vantage. You emerge near "Little Rec," the children's ball grounds, traditionally the site of Easter egg hunts and May festivals. Skirt the lawn, then swing south with the walk to enter Children's Playground.

A happy burst of color and a series of big interrelated circles appear through the gap in surrounding hedges as you walk into the playground. On your right, faced by some handsome new benches, is the tot lot, a site chosen for the littlest children because it is the warmest part of the playground. Walk toward it. Where possible, old equipment, such as the classic swings, has been repaired and repainted. The salvaged is interlarded with imaginative new equipment, for example, a mouse tower to climb, a sturdy pole teeter-totter, a platform to stand on, and a trolls' bridge to crawl through that should recall *Three Billy Goats Gruff* to most of us.

When Park and Recreation Department General Manager Jack Spring took me with him on his walk of inspection of the redesigned playground, he recalled that this area was "the donkey track where I started my first job in the park. I was twelve years old and worked four hours a day for fifteen cents an hour. May Day 1931 was my first day," he recalls, "and I led a goat cart bearing the Queen of the May in a procession. The following days weren't so glamorous. I followed the donkeys with a shovel."

A boat ride concession, and later sandboxes, replaced the donkey track. As you come around the circle enclosing the tot lot, walk south toward the highest point of the area. Playground supervisor Tom Bass says a group of adult gymnasts headed by Captain George Neise of the fire department work out regularly on the parallel bars here. So do a number of aspiring would-be Olga Korbuts. Across from the gymnasts' circle, slide fanciers should be delighted with the big center circle, designed for older children. It has retained the great old spiral slides, the short bumpy slides, and added some tall new ones. Climb the hillside with the walkway to get an overview of the complex with its swinging bridge, the refurbished rocking circle swings, and an amazing log jungle gym. From this vantage, one can also discover how sensitively landscape designer Michael Painter has used space and plant materials to complement the wonderful old carousel. The carousel and its animals have been repainted and renovations are underway on the burned Sharon Cottage, the big Romanesque building that forms a backdrop to the playground.

Stroll downhill from the big slide toward the little farm, recently reshingled. Children can now go into the yard and associate with the animals, just as they do at Children's Zoo. Then walk toward the bridge that overlooks the new river-rock cobbled pool. The waterfall uses recycled water. Stand awhile on the bridge to survey this happy scene. Old-timers who miss the totem poles that once stood on the far hillside may be sad, as Jack Spring is, that "like all wooden things, they finally went back to the soil. If anyone has a totem pole to donate, we'd welcome it."

A pyramid-shaped monument indicating that the reconstruction is a "Gift of Love" to Miss Connally from two former park commission presidents, Walter Haas and Walter Shorenstein, has gone in near the bridge. When you have had your fill of the colorful scene, walk from Hammond Valley, which fronts on Sharon Cottage, across the parking lot to find the lawn bowling greens and the clubhouse John McLaren built for bowlers. Then to complete this walk, follow Bowling Green Drive and walk northeasterly to reach the tennis courts. An underpass is just beyond the clubhouse. Follow it under the drive to emerge at Favorite Point, where the second underpass dips below the park's main drive to come out in Conservatory Valley.

Children are welcome to pet the animals in the little farm.

View from the cement slides in Children's Playground.

After you have enjoyed the poinsettias, azaleas, and cyclamen, follow John F. Kennedy Drive east to McLaren Lodge. Traditionally, the lights go on on the big tree on McLaren's birthday, December 20. During his lifetime, pipers playing light Scottish airs were also a tradition. After you have admired the big tree, with or without lights, walk past it to Stanyan Street and bear right to return to the point of origin, and public transportation, at Haight Street, closing this circle walk.

14

Enjoy the Treasures of Science

The treasures of science await any child in San Francisco at a compound of templelike buildings located in Golden Gate Park and known as the California Academy of Sciences. The academy is located in Golden Gate Park, facing the Music Concourse. It is open daily from 10:00 A.M. until 5:00 P.M. The 10 Monterey bus stops across the concourse from the academy.

The collected wonders of the natural world, including bushtits, humuhumunukunukuapuaa, oryx, dik-diks, gerunuks, pterodactyls, klipspringers, zeines, and an axolotl in a bottle, are all to be seen here. So is Kipling's bicolored python rock snake with the scalesome, flailsome tail and 96,999 more reptiles, 31,000 more fish, 3,626,000 bugs, 300,000 mounted plants, 1,600,000 fossils, and an awesome seven-figure book collection.

They could not all be looked at intelligibly by one person in a hundred days. So, since the academy is mostly indoors, charges a modest admission fee, and always has something additional to see, the stroll through it has become, without question, the favorite rainy-day walk for thousands, including teachers, preachers, fathers, mothers, brothers, and others whose broods get broody when the ground gets wet.

It could also be called, without hesitation, the thinking man's walk. Thinking is half of what makes the academy valuable to our time and to our town, as well as what makes it fun. The other half is seeing.

To see the academy, you must begin this walk at the Music Concourse. Walk through the new wing to the court containing Robert Howard's statue of mating whales, which sometimes spouts water and has become a hallmark for the complex surrounding it. North American Hall, built in 1924, is the south

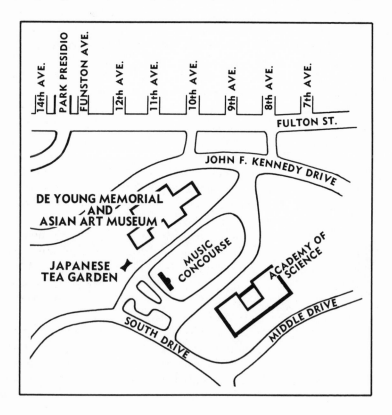

side; Morrison Planetarium, completed in 1951, is the north side, and Steinhart Aquarium, which dates from 1926, the center building.

For the first-time visitor, the planetarium door is the best choice. Go through it and walk straight ahead to Lovell White Hall. On one side of the arch is a map of the buildings (near the planetarium ticket booth). On the other side is a blue display case labeled "Exhibit of the Month." At one time it contained a collection of gastroliths. To the initiated these are the gizzard stones of dinosaurs. If it hadn't occurred to you that prehistoric beasts had crops, like chickens, you have just discovered the kind of surprise that brings 2.5 million people through these doors every year. The seven men who started the California Academy of Sciences in Lewis Sloat's office, 129 Montgomery Street, in 1853, could not possibly have known that intellectual curiosity would one day make their effort outstanding, but it has.

At the terminus of Lovell White Hall is African Hall, which includes a two-horned African rhino, a gift of the late Dean Witter, financier and hunter. Also at the terminus is the Alice Eastwood Hall of Botany, jutting off to the right. One ever-changing exhibit of fresh California native plants carries on a tradition started by the plucky woman botanist who saved the academy's herbarium, then at 822 Market, from the 1906 fire. Another popular display is the section of giant redwood tree, which has been enhanced by an electrical system that shows what size the tree was in 1066.

African Hall makes a square around the auditorium, and by bearing ever left the walker will be brought out into the main corridor again. Walk toward the Foucault Pendulum or "Time Ball," which swings in a constant demonstration of the rotation of the earth. It is the landmark for Morrison Planetarium. Times for the star shows are posted on the door.

It is possible to enter either the Hall of Man or the aquarium near the pendulum. A small hallway furnished with benches and a soft-drink machine gives onto a pit swamp, where the alligators, like ambulant logs, drowse sleepily. But that is another walk.

15

A Safari Under Glass

This is the age of the safari. If postcards from friends, travel ads, or the Gold Drum catalog, which used to offer live baby elephants and tiger and leopard kittens for gift giving, are any indication, it's the Green Hills of Africa or you're out of it, bwana.

The next best thing, especially on a rainy day, is a vicarious safari through the Simson African Hall at the California Academy of Sciences.

Humming Saint Saens' "Carnival of Animals," begin this walk at the door to the left of the *Mating Whales,* a fountain by sculptor Robert Howard, which was prominently displayed at the 1939 World's Fair on Treasure Island and has now come to be the signature of the academy.

Between a sign which says Morrison Planetarium on one side and Hall of Science on the other, walk in, climb the few steps, and turn left.

In a few steps you are in Africa. You can tell by the hyena and the warthog in cases on the left. Between them is a pangolin, an armor-plated anteater considered sacred by some African tribes. How would you like to find a land snail, like his neighbor, who may weigh up to a pound, loose in the agapanthus some morning?

The next specimen on your right is not a member of the Fugs nor the Animals. To meet him on the hoof you would have had to go to the Birunga Mountains, north of Lake Kivu in the Congo. Like the creatures in the dioramas in the hall immediately right, he has stood here since 1934 when the African Hall, a gift of Leslie Simson, a native San Franciscan mining engineer and sportsman, was dedicated.

In ten steps you are in Simson African Hall proper, fitted like a railroad station with generous benches. Sit awhile among the bush bucks, lechwes, oribis, and zebras, squint into the distance and you can travel from Kenya to the Cape, or Kilimanjaro to the Sahara. Any of the gazellelike animals would make a good meal for that pride of lions overlooking the veldt at sunset.

Or if high fashion interests you, look at the simian wimian among the Colobus monkeys across from the cheetah. Notice the nitpicker on the neck of the giraffe at the water hole.

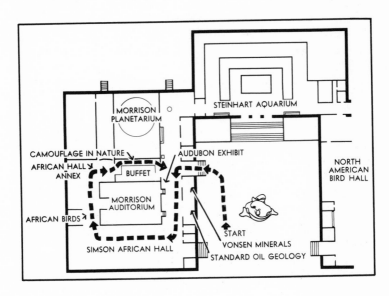

Bear right to see an exhibit that shows how skins are re-created on an armature, rather than "stuffed," and the meticulous handwork on grass and leaves.

Immediately beyond is a section devoted to African birds,

Fashion has been inspired by the Colobus monkey.

which tells the story of parallel evolution. Notice the red-winged blackbird of America and its splendid African counterpart, the long-tailed whydah.

If you thought the bongo was a drum, look across the corridor as one prepares to take a drink. Then to get the real thrill of the safari, turn into Lovell White Hall.

Here the game is to go hunting with your eyes. Two points for the praying mantis that looks like an orchid. Two for the spider who could be a buttercup. Ten for the viper, if you see him at all.

Since trophies are often the object of a safari, end this walk at any of the academy bookstands, where the low-priced rock, shells, and scientific artifacts make a worthy windup for any trek.

16

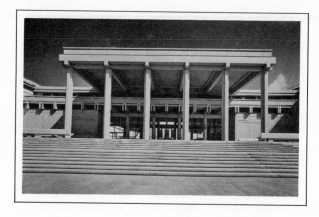

The Wattis Hall of Man

. . . they remained everywhere the same—the
animal who remade its world. . . .

Bruce Finson

Under an eye-fooling sky of mirrored black infinity, Man, the planetary animal, has been captured like a trophy and displayed on shelves at the elegant anthropological wing of the California Academy of Sciences. It is called, not the Parliament of, nor the Palace of, as earlier periods might more grandiloquently have named it, but quite simply the Wattis Hall of Man. There, in tableau after tableau, we—or at least some of our alter egos—are planting rice, drying fish, digging yams, weaving mats, surveying a recently slain seal—doing all those interesting things we do to feed, clothe, comfort, and amuse ourselves.

If you haven't been out to see it, go. Where else in San

Francisco can you stroll from the tropics to the Artic by way of Japan or Australia?

Short of replication, or being born there, there are two ways to get into the Wattis Hall of Man: The sneaky way is via a back entrance off Middle Drive (a little east of South Drive) where a two-lane road has been widened and repaved to permit entrance to the anthropology wing via two stunning galleries. One is named for Atholl McBean, the other for Patricia Price Peterson, and they are designed to house traveling exhibits between great windows that look out on greenery. You can pay your fifty cents here and be inside Wattis Hall of Man in twenty steps.

The other way in is through the big glassy main entrance that faces the Music Concourse of Golden Gate Park. If you go on a Sunday between 10:00 A.M. and 5:00 P.M., using the Muni 78 shuttlebus, which brings people into the park from Stanyan and Frederick streets near Kezar Stadium, the front entrance is the one that is handy. The shuttle stops and picks up at McLaren Lodge, the Conservatory, the Music Concourse, the Japanese Tea Garden, the de Young Museum and the Academy of Sciences, so walkers who weary can plan park excursions with these handy pickup points in mind.

From the main entrance hall, walk resolutely away for the moment from that enticing new gift and book shop, note in passing that the stairs lead down to the academy buffet, and head to the left through the auditorium archway. Make a right turn and you are in the Edward Hohfeld Hall of Space Science. Continue past the planetarium until you are at the pendulum. Weight watchers may want to pause to give themselves a thrill with a slight digression to the right here. On two adjacent scales, it is possible to compare one's earth weight and lunar weight. One six-foot five-inch man, I observed, weighed 198 pounds terrestrial but would only be 33 pounds 3 ounces moon weight. Get off the moon scale, do an about face and you are headed into the Wattis Gallery, a long narrow display area that could currently send collectors, chefs, decorators, and gourmets into raptures over the Elkus Collection of Navajo rugs, Indian

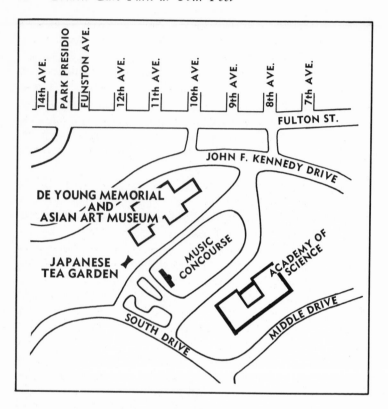

jewelry, and katchina dolls, and the overlapping Reitz Collection of cooking paraphernalia gathered around the world. To see it best, bear left and browse one side, then return via the opposite wall. This technique will bring you right back to the grander entrance to the Wattis Hall of Man.

Step inside and it's how now brown room! Already big, the illusion of infinity makes it seem endless in any direction. Here again, the technique for seeing it most easily is to bear left, away from the big Paleolithic right wall given over to stones and bones, past the half-moon of stage where ethnic dances are often performed. Head toward the boar who looks ready to charge the New Guinea native digging yams. If the latter took a few steps forward, he could spear some interesting glass cases of his life's treasures, all displayed so the littlest tot can see them as well as the rest of us.

Meander on to the Caroline Islands, where a Micronesian under a palm tree is plaiting mats near an outrigger canoe. Japan is next and in a seven-league-booted leap, there are the kayak and stilt house of a West Coast Alaskan Eskimo that could be Ugaligmiut, Magemiut, Kuskowagamiut, or Togiagamiut. No one is in sight. Are they all whooping it up at the Malamiut saloon?

At the end of the hall you reach a display of inland or Netsilik Eskimo in the cold desert, complete with local snow. (The baby seal was once stolen from the academy, possibly for ransom, and later turned up in San Rafael.) The fashion conscious will be surprised to find that the hunter is wearing caribou skins in his parka, not a woven alpaca blanket, while kids will love the sled dog, snowshoes, and face masks.

Start back past the space reserved for herders of the high Andes, hitting the Southwest Hopi display, and you are on your way from cold desert to hot desert where the Australian Abos "chase the rain." The big center display is the wikiup of the Yurok Indian of northern California, so cleverly arranged that you feel like you're right inside with the smoke, the skins, and the fish drying.

There is more to come, presently in preparation. Next to be finished will be a display of Navajos, followed by camel herders of East Africa. Not yet in the planning stage, alas, is the display I miss and keep hoping for: A model anthropologist complete with tent, tape recorder, binoculars, camera, pith helmet, and Land Rover. In the foreground, bending over a Coleman magic kitchen, would be the native person of choice, eager to please and looking up with the obvious question, "Kundalini make tiffin?"

17

The Aquarium—a Fine Show

If you can't go down to the sea in scuba gear, the next best thing is a walk in Steinhart Aquarium.

Imagine strolling around an undersea Union Square with windows that might have been done by Salvador Dali or Picasso. Or going to a ballet choreographed by Dante. Or watching a peep show revealing secrets of the sea we land livers forgot in the ancient Silurian time, 350 million years ago, when the first pioneer arthropod put an exploratory foot up on shore.

That's Steinhart. No show in the city can top it.

To savor this expedition to the fullest, choose an otherwise drab day. Then seek out the Academy of Sciences, which is located east of the Music Concourse in Golden Gate Park, about where Ninth Avenue would spear it, if it went straight through.

The tremendous columns behind the statue of dancing whales have beckoned aquarists since 1923, when Ignatz Steinhart's gift to San Francisco was built.

Once past the columns, you arrive immediately at the balustrade of a remarkable tropical garden complete with waterfall. This is the great pit swamp where 250-pound alligators snooze or cruise in the ooze. It is also a wishing pond where gathered coins help buy new fish for the aquarium.

Not long ago a visitor from Sweden, carried away by generosity or remorse, dropped her alligator handbag into the swamp. One of the resident 'gators, perhaps recognizing a relative, swam over and hooked the strap on his neck. Handlers managed to retrieve a soggy Swedish passport. Those who wish to look for crocodile tears will find crocodiles in the smaller pond on the left.

Go to the right and down two steps for a look at the world of reptiles and amphibians. The blue-tailed skinks, Russell's viper, the ghostly ajolote, the lizardy Knight anole, the Tokay gecko; an emerald tree boa that looks like a droopy green stomacher designed for Tiffany's; a great blobby toad called the Blomberg; and the tiny green poison frog whose venom is used for tipping arrows in the jungle; all live here.

As you come out of the turnstile that does the counting, keep to your right. In a few minutes you will be abreast of a

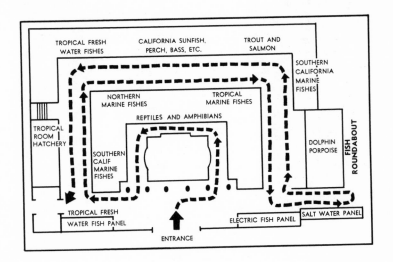

tank of anchovies. Caesar salad on the fin in a whirlpool bath. Walk another step or two to press the button for a finny symphony. Modern atonal music has nothing on the spotfin and yellowfin croakers, Steinhart's famous "talking fishes." Tidepools that empty and refill to demonstrate wave action on the

The colorful tropical fishes at Steinhart Aquarium.

resident anemones and sea urchins are another of the never-ending shows.

Look among the tropical marine fishes for the Moorish idol, striped brown, yellow, and white, with an extravagant dorsal fin. This is Steinhart's symbol. Nearby is the meanest fish in the aquarium, the giant sea bass, *Epinephelus itajara*. When he came from Florida many years ago, he was twelve inches long. Now he is about four feet long and attacks anything put in his tank except the little blue cleanerfish. Like the tickbirds that clean the African hippos and rhinos, the cleanerfish police up his gills and teeth.

Before you swing around the corner to look at Cissie, the orphaned harbor seal, as she flirts among the white-sided dolphins, step down the hall to see tanks of jewellike little fish, including the three spot damsel and the striped sweetlips.

The deadly stonefish, the turkeyfish, the hairy decorator crabs who dress up in seaweed pasted on with spittle, the sea-feathers that puff up like a ballerina's tutu, and the tropical angler, who walks and has a built-in fly rod, are also here.

Then plunge back into the quadrangle of tanks for a look at Whiskers, the fresh-water dolphin. There are 10,000 other residents, among them the clown loaches, the aholeholes, the uluakihikihi as well as the perches, the pikes, the sharks, and the eels, to meet in this fine kettle of fish.

18

Fish Roundabout

USED TROUT STREAM FOR SALE.
MUST BE SEEN TO BE APPRECIATED. . . .

*i went up close and looked at the length of the
stream. I could see some trout in them. I saw one
good fish. I saw some crawdads crawling around
the rocks at the bottom. . . . It looked like a fine
stream. I put my hand in the water. It was cold
and felt good. . . .*

> Richard Brautigan
> *Trout Fishing in America*

March 5, 1978

Dear Richard:

Thanks for your check for $39.97, which pays up the last of
your calls to Japan on my telephone. It came just in time to buy
a new umbrella, which I have need of lately.

As you may remember, it has been my lifelong ambition to fish Brooks Hall, one of the few places in San Francisco where a person can stand surrounded on all sides by water held back only by a wall. Standing as it does in the bed of Yerba Buena Creek, you could probably whack a pickax through and get water. Not that I am sure there are any fish left there, or even any blind newts, because you can't see them when you park your car. I have decided to give up trying to figure out how to fish Brooks Hall, though, because during the recent drought somebody at City Hall had the good sense to reopen the Civic Center well for cooling their big computer. I certainly wouldn't want that computer to start running a temperature until after tax time.

My new fishing ambition has moved a couple miles west. Aside from Alex Guinness and maybe Melina Mercouri (remember Topkapi), I can't think of anyone but you who could help me realize it. I only hope that out of our long friendship, you will give it some thought. Believe me, the project will call for cunning, courage, and imagination. Instead of Brooks Hall, I now aspire to fish the new Fish Roundabout at the Academy of Sciences!

If you haven't heard about it up there in Montana, imagine having a captive ocean in your closet. This Fish Roundabout is a wall of water. You stand in the middle of it and can see right through the plastic wall. Believe me, it is loaded with fish. Like, would you believe dozens of yellowfins and jacks. Mackerel. Bass. Big twenty-six and thirty pounders. Three feet long, if they're an inch. Even sharks. Swimming in schools, they race around you like stock cars at Sears Point. My God, Richard, with the right gear and bait, a fisherman could pull in his limit in ten minutes. Maybe six. Except that I haven't figured out where to cast from. Scuba gear may be the only way to go. I thought of taking a trident but the Plexiglas is three inches thick. Also, any puncture would dampen the rug.

If you want to case this place, take any bus out to Golden Gate Park and go to the Music Concourse off Kennedy Drive, parallel to about Eighth Avenue. You know where all those gnarly sycamore trees are lined up like a regiment of Spanish-American War vets at parade rest? Well, the big building on the south side, the one that looks like a savings and loan or an empty department store that somehow floated out here from downtown on an astral high tide, is the Academy of Sciences. If you don't recognize it, it's probably because the old landmark statue of Francis Scott Key that used to sit near the millstones at the entrance to the academy is now at the east end of the Music Concourse where he can hear the national anthem.

It'll cost you to go into the academy, of course, but look on it as an investment, like your fishing license. When you get into the big main entrance hall, for just a moment you may think you have been trapped in a special "people-quarium" for air-breathing fishes of the future to view a few captive hominids left over from the twentieth century. Don't let it throw you. Walk firmly toward the courtyard where Bob Howard's *Mating Whales* should bring you back to familiar reality. When you spot the classic columns of Steinhart Aquarium, go up the steps between them. Bear right at the swamp. I usually stop here and wink at a big crocodile with whom I've been carrying on a long friendship since the day I saw him swallow a set of car keys a man dropped over the side. (Any foe of fossil fuel is a friend of mine.) But don't feel you have to visit with him on my account. You could plan to return later to see him and the turtles, snakes, lizards, frogs, newts, dolphins, harbor seals, clown loaches, flashlight fish, and that big cantankerous bass at your leisure.

For this expedition, go past the men's room. Suddenly, there you are at the Fish Roundabout, surrounded by a swirl of cement like the lower level of the Oakland Coliseum or the O'Farrell Street garage. This is it! A surreal indoor ocean approached by wall-to-wall carpeting. Above the Guggenheim upward swirl of ramp is a big round doughnut of real salt sea, 10 feet wide, 204 feet in circumference, a captive river racing about at the speed of the Humboldt Current. They say there are two more like it in Japan, but I haven't seen them.

To engender the proper ocean viewing mood, there is a rocky mock pond on the first floor. Sort of a round haiku of tidepool called a touch tank. Usually it swarms with kids. A young woman docent who sits on one side keeps telling them,

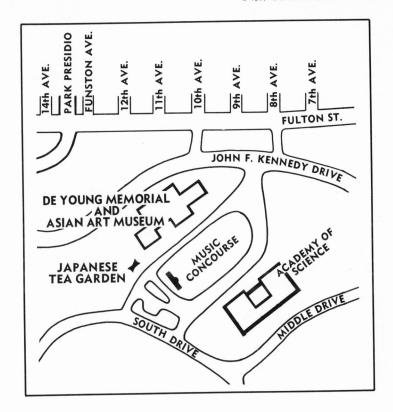

"Yes, you can put your hand in and touch the small creatures if you are careful."

I put my pinky up to a sea anemone and it gave me a French kiss. I don't think we should let this information get around though, or there will be all sorts of weirdos down there taking advantage of those little sea anemones.

Once you've indulged in this mental decompression chamber, letting the mundane vibes slide off your jacket down past the starfish into the water, or onto the wall-to-wall, you are ready for bigger things. Go up the ramp and whoooooosh! In thirty steps, give or take a few, there you are full fathoms five in the deep gray sea without a wet suit or casting pole. I mean, man, it could frustrate the most serene fisherman to see all those big babies swirling past like they were inside the Twentieth Century Limited club car. And there you stand, both inside and outside the action. Missed the train. Left standing in the station dry as Kansas.

If you get any inspirations on how to fish this place, please let me know.

Come to think of it, before you leave the academy there is something else new and fishy there you'll want to see. It's Old Blue Eyes, the coelacanth, *Latimeria chalumnae*, they call the living fossil. Except this one isn't living. He's swimming in formaldehyde and has a whole fan club named for him. They call it SPOOF, the Society for Preservation of Old Fish.

As Ever,

Margot Patterson Doss

19

Search the Treasure Trove

For all loved Art in a seemly way
With an earnest soul and a capital A. . . .

James Jeffrey Roche

The M. H. de Young Memorial Museum in Golden Gate Park is San Francisco's oldest and largest fine arts museum. There is no way a walker can digest all the treasures on display within its 200,000 feet of floor space in one day. This, of course, is part of the durable charm. Quite aside from the ever-changing important traveling shows, whenever one goes to the de Young, there is always something new to discover.

An ideal time to visit is when the neighboring Japanese Tea Garden is in its springtime glory. The convenient way to go is via public transportation. To make this walk, take Muni bus 5, 10, or 16 to Fulton Street at either Eighth or Tenth Avenue. From either corner, go to the south side of Fulton. Look for a diagonal walkway that goes into the park heading toward an underpass that tunnels beneath Kennedy Drive parallel to Ninth Avenue. This shortcut, cleverly contrived to bring walkers into the California International Midwinter Fair of 1894 without danger from horse-drawn equipage, serves just as safely in our time. It brings the walker out of a green and pleasant lane to emerge alongside the museum. Distance: barely the length of a nearby city block.

When you emerge, bear right facing the Music Concourse on Tea Garden Drive. In a trice you will be approaching the charming Pool of Enchantment, a water garden with sculpture of mountain lions and an Indian boy by Earl Cummings. Often abloom with water lilies, the pool mirrors the 134-foot tower over the main entrance. When initially designed in 1917 by architect Louis Mullgardt, the building was much more Spanish

Mandalas and sculpture in the Indian galleries.

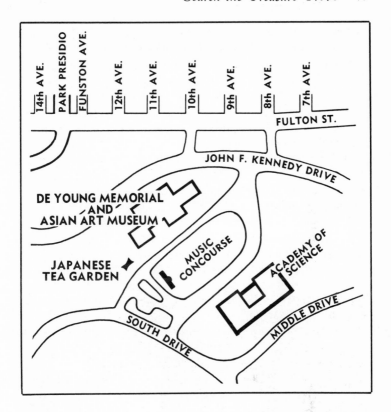

and churrigueresque. It replaced an earlier building from the Midwinter Exposition. Wings were added in 1925, 1931, and more recently, in 1964. The newest addition accommodates the Asian Art Museum, better known as the Brundage Collection. Bliss, Hurt, Trudell, and Berger were the architects who modernized the face of the older building, cleaning it of decoration in a remodeling in 1950.

Once through the main entrance, stop and look about you to sort out the foyer clutter of transitory desks. In this maze, the admission desk is right of the door, a checkroom desk across from it. Volunteers man an information desk across the hall, flanked on either side of the forecourt by bookstores. Go into the new Egyptian gift and bookstore and you may discover that The Maltese Falcon was really Horus.

For a first-time exploration of the museum, walk straight ahead from the main entrance through the forecourt until you are at the steps of the Hearst Court, a tremendous room hung with distinguished tapestries, often the scene of concerts and lectures. Plan to come back and inspect the imposing monastery entrance at the far side, but for the moment stop short of the steps and bear right.

When you are abreast of the little round gallery displaying decorative wallpaper of savages of the Pacific, go in to see a fanciful representation Sir Francis Drake would have appreciated. Beyond is a lovely federal period parlor out of New England, suitable for Old Wasps at Home. It is one of a succession of well-decorated rooms of various historical periods interspersed with galleries from significant periods of European art. In my private fantasy, by night these are peopled with courtly types who disappear, either to the sub-subbasement or Transylvania at sunrise.

Return to the umbilical corridor and when you reach the high chest of drawers, nicknamed Bette Midler by one wit, bear right into the American Galleries toward the tremendous portrait of the father of our country. Notice how Washington's watch fob matches his horse's tail, a detail that often brings a smile to viewers. Around the corner, to the right, Californiana buffs will be delighted to find Leland Stanford picnicking behind some beautifully costumed guests in a glassed-in niche. Prize painting of the nineteenth-century collection is the *Rape of the Sabine Women*. Notice how the adjoining ancestors look discreetly away, seemingly making social commentary on that era. My own favorite of Charles C. Nahl's work is his portrait of a Sacramento Indian. There is also a fine William Hahn cityscape of the old Sacramento train station. When you have sought out the famous Harnett *After the Hunt* and the Alexander Pope *Trumpeter Swan*, two among many fine American paintings, if it is near lunch time, retrace your steps to the hallway, bear right until you are at Gallery 21, devoted to British art, and head for

The Louis XV room is part of the Roscoe and Margaret Oakes collection.

the Cafe de Young. At its entrance is a bust of M. H. de Young himself, originator of both the museum and the Midwinter Fair, genial as Colonel Sanders. Someone had placed a fresh carnation in his buttonhole when I was there last. In India, such a benefactor would have a wreath of flowers made from freshly torn *San Francisco Chronicles* placed around his neck daily.

Once refreshed, it is the better part of wisdom to leave the Kress Galleries, the rooms and galleries devoted to the ancient world, the Middle Ages, the Renaissance, to Spain, to Italy, to Africa, Oceania, and the Americas for another visit, lest input overload obscure your appreciation. But since Gardner Dailey, architect of the Brundage wing, built in a special two-stage springtime pleasure, leave yourself time to seek out on the first floor, left off the far end of Adrian Gruen Court, the big window in the Osgood Hooker gallery. It was specially placed and enlarged to give an intimate look into the neighboring Japanese

Tea Garden. When you have absorbed its sweet serenity, go up to the second floor, immediately above it (in the gallery devoted to Momoyana and Edo ceramics), for another look at the same scene from the upper window. This broader view makes the garden approximate a segment of Japanese village.

Then leave the museum to visit the Tea Garden itself. Go in through its nearest gate and out through the western side gate. Take a sharp right here and you will be on another shortcut. This one leads past the old monastery stones to Kennedy Drive. Cross it by the Rose Garden and bear right to return to your starting place.

20

An Oasis of Oriental Charm

After eighty years of almost continual daily use, the Japanese Tea Garden, next to the de Young Museum in Golden Gate Park, could still ask "Mirror, mirror, on the wall, which is the fairest on the mall?" with assurance that the right sycophantic answer would be forthcoming.

Planted originally by George Turner Marsh as the Japanese Village of the Midwinter Exposition of 1894, enlarged with a "Peace" lantern and garden given in 1953 by Japanese cities, renewed even more recently through the efforts of the late Mrs. Frank Gerbode and the San Francisco Garden Club, the Tea Garden is the most exquisite three acres in the park. It is also the most popular, as busload after busload of visitors can attest.

For many of them, it is all they will ever know of Japan. For others, it is a way to recapture Kyoto. Whatever the reason for the visit, the Tea Garden does not disappoint them, for, like any good garden in Japan, there is more here than meets the eye. Plants, plans, artifacts, skills, and laborers were all imported to create authentically this oasis from a mundane world. The unities, verities, and a few of the foibles of a thousand years of gardening arts are all at work to delight and refresh the stroller.

In a way, the Tea Garden is a temple. Not as in redwood groves, which are by coincidence Gothic cathedrals, but by design in the Buddhist way, which is that man and nature are one. Any alert walker will realize, as soon as he goes through either gate, that his connection with the outside world is broken. And so he should, for he is on the *roji,* the garden path to the teahouse, and also, as Kakuzo Okakura describes it in the *Book of Tea,* en route to "the first stage of meditation—the passage into self-illumination."

If this seems an ambitious route to travel on a morning's walk, all the Tea Garden really requires is that a walker put one foot in front of the other and follow the path. It leads beside still waters, over the irregularities of stepping stones, under the dappled light that filters through evergreens, past moss-covered granite lanterns to reflecting pools, a teahouse, a moonbridge, a Buddha. The paths are irresistible. Something beckons beyond each bend. Around each corner something evermore enticing presents itself. For the knowledgeable, the symbolic rectangle, triangle, and circle can be discerned from each contemplation bench, although sometimes the viewer is the circle.

Long ago, the family of Makota Hagiwara lived in the Tea Garden, maintained it, baked the tea cookies, fed the carp, prepared and served the tea, and at least one member died here, all in a manner suitable to the highest traditions of the Grand Kabuki theater. An exquisite Ruth Asawa plaque left of the main entrance salutes the Hagiwara family's contribution. When the War Department relocation exiled San Francisco's Japanese population, a dashing Australian, Alan Agnew, and his wife became hosts. Today, Japanese are again hosts at the teahouse and giftshop. Park department gardeners feed the carp, clip the *bonsai,* prune the cherry trees, and clean the coins from beneath "the wishing bridge."

To find the Buddha "that sits through sunny and rainy weather without shade," walk uphill from the teahouse. This is *Amazarashi-no-hotoke-Buddha,* cast in 1790 in Tajima ken, Japan, and it is reputed to the largest Buddha ever imported—a gift to the park in 1949 from Gump's.

With the five-tiered, wooden Shinto pagoda as a landmark, walk away from the *tori* to locate the "Peace" lantern and garden regarded as modern in Japan. The style is Muromachi, only

The cherry trees are seas of bloom in the Tea Garden.

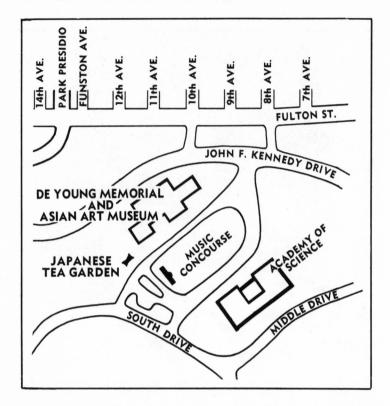

500 years old. While the rest of the Tea Garden has *sabi,* an appearance of antiquity, rusticity, and emphasis on natural textures, the new garden is known rather for *wabi,* a sense of quietness, astringency, good taste, and tranquility.

If you don't dig it all the first time you walk it, like Zen, try again.

21

The Monastery in the Park

Golden Gate Park has many surprises. One of the more astonishing is a Forgotten Works, to borrow a phrase from Richard Brautigan's surreal novel, *In Watermelon Sugar*.

An uninformed walker who stumbles unwittingly upon this Forgotten Works, a field of tremendous hand-chiseled stones, moss covered and charred and laying in the tall grass, might puzzle and speculate upon them endlessly. Actually, as long-time residents of San Francisco know, the great stones are the disassembled ruin of El Monasterio de Santa Maria de Avila, begun by monks of the Cistercian Order in the twelfth century on the banks of the Tagus River eighty miles northeast of Madrid, Spain.

Part of the ruin has been reconstructed within the M. H. de Young Memorial Museum, and a walk to see the stone yard and the reconstruction can be a pleasant Sunday excursion. En route one also discovers a good shortcut from Kennedy Drive to the Music Concourse.

Begin this walk at Tenth Avenue and Fulton Street. Start into the park on the west side of the street and take the path that leads off on your right through Heroes' Grove, a fifteen-acre tract of redwood trees dedicated by the Gold Star Mothers of San Francisco to their sons and daughters slain in World War I. These redwoods, gardeners will notice, are oddly short, but beneath them one still finds that special cathedral stillness. In the rainy season, one may also find an unexpected pond in the little canyon.

At a stream head, which seems to come in from under Kennedy Drive, you will emerge from the grove near the Rose Garden. Cross the drive. Look for a sign at the roadside behind the M. H. de Young Memorial Museum. It begins with Japanese Tea Garden, lists five more of the park attractions fronting the Music Concourse, and ends Pedestrians Only. Follow this macadam path fifty yards south. Suddenly there is an odd piece of masonry at the side of the trail. Take a few more steps and you have reached the Forgotten Works.

Walk in and look at the intricate sculpture, the rosettes and scrollwork of the long unused pediments and columns. Before you let your civic indignation rise that these beautiful pieces should rest here unappreciated, reflect on three factors: The ruin was not a complete structure when it was shipped here. It had been deconsecrated for a hundred years and was in use, unroofed, as a stable at the time of its purchase. Do we really want any more buildings in Golden Gate Park, anyway?

The story behind the migrant monastery is more enjoyable when one has answered that last consideration negatively. It began in 1930 when Arthur Byne, an American authority on Spanish architecture, discovered the ruin in the hands of an aristocratic family that had been friendly to the Crown in 1834 when the Cistercians were evicted by royal edict. The roof tiles had long since been appropriated by poor peasants and the refectory was in use as a manure storage pit. Byne bought the stones and sold them to William Randolph Hearst, who hired Walter Steilberg, a Berkeley architect, to superintend the demo-

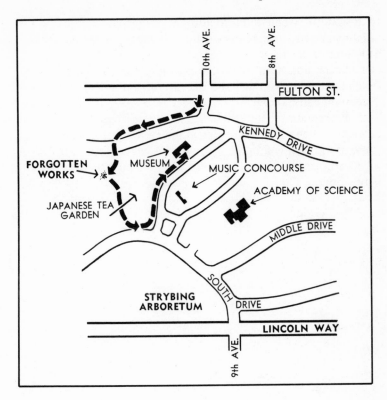

lition, a job that took eight months and included building a
road to the Tagus to transport the stones—a 100-yard, inclined,
narrow-gauge railway to the river—and commandeering the
entire excelsior supply of Spain for a while. The ruin got out of
Spain just a week before King Alfonso VIII was crowned, only
to spend ten years in a Haslett waterfront warehouse.

The Great Depression of the thirties changed Hearst's plan
to reconstruct the building at his 67,000-acre summer place on
the McCloud River, and instead he sold the 1,500 crates of stone
to the city of San Francisco. In the intervening time, while a
succession of mayors have been unable to decide where to put

the stones of contention, there have been five incidents in the last twenty-two years when the crates have caught fire. Hence the char on some of these stones.

When you have pondered at length, continue south on the path and soon you will be abreast of the side gates of the Japanese Tea Garden.

If secondary uses of the stones interest you, take a good look too at the stepping stones in the Japanese Tea Garden and also at the wall within the Garden of Fragrance in nearby Strybing Arboretum. These stones seem to be creeping south, somehow.

22

Everybody's Garden

Strybing Arboretum, one of the rare, unique walks of San Francisco, is an expert's paradise in an age of expertise.

From the Tuileries to Kew, and from Kew to Kyoto, it is known in leafy circles for the number and variety of plants it can, and does, grow outdoors. In addition to plants native to our own hemisphere, the seventy acres of Strybing Arboretum successfully harbor the plants of China, Japan, the Himalayas, South America, Central America, Australia, Burma, New Zealand, and South Africa.

The *Davidia involucrata* or dove tree, the *Magnolia campbellii* and the *Michelia doltsopa* are but three of the rarities that bring visitors from all over the world to Strybing. This corner of Golden Gate Park is also so beautiful, so secret and quiet, that anyone who needs to escape the pressures of today may do so among the botanical treasures.

A walker could be led down Strybing's garden paths daily and make new discoveries every time. The place to start is at

Ninth Avenue and Lincoln Way, where the Garden Center and Hall of Flowers is located. This building, finished in 1960, is one of the few municipal structures taxpayers can enjoy without feeling their hackles rise, for it was purchased painlessly with pari-mutuel racing funds.

The San Francisco Flower Show, our county fair, formerly held in the rotunda of City Hall, blossoms here annually the fourth week in August. Twenty of the city's garden clubs and flower societies pool their talents to produce the show, biggest of many held in the Garden Center and open to exhibitors in the nine Bay Area counties.

The wrought-iron gates at the north end of the building are now the main entrance to Strybing Arboretum. The other entrance is located on South Drive near the Japanese Tea Garden and has a turnstile that can let visitors out if they are caught

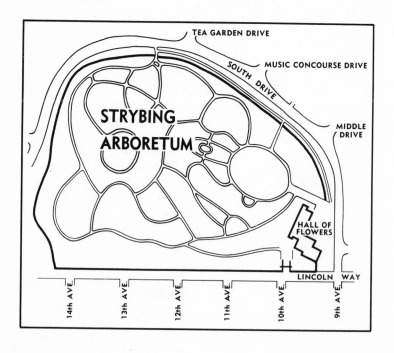

after the arboretum is locked at 4:30 P.M. on weekdays and 5:00 P.M. on weekends.

Walking toward it around the perimeter of the arboretum, you will pass two gardens. One, a series of demonstration gardens covering two and a half acres, shows San Franciscans how to design and grow a successful garden in the climate and soil common to their own backyards. The other is the Garden of Fragrance for the blind.

This garden, plus one of medicinal plants and another of California natives, was part of the stipulation in the bequest of the late Mrs. Christian M. Strybing, who left $100,000 to create a public arboretum when she died in 1926. Helene Strybing also left the city six emeralds and a handful of rare coins, thereby creating one of our long-time unsolved puzzles. The emeralds, appraised after banging around City Hall for eighteen years in a brass-bound box, turned out to be glass, while the coins were judged to be worth $48.

Near the main entrance there used to be rhododendrons planted by the late Eric Walther, the eccentric first director of the arboretum. Look to the left to find the first tree planted in the arboretum, *Drimys winteri,* named for one of Sir Francis Drake's captains. Bearing west, the walker will come upon an information booth where it is possible to purchase plant guides and get directions. Following a westerly path that loops downhill twice and circles back to the information booth, the walker will pass five exciting planting areas installed in more recent years. These include the redwood grove, paid for by the Hillsborough Garden Club; the California section, and the Noble conifer collection. All are well labeled.

In a city of fewer splendors, Strybing Arboretum would be loudly touted. Though largely unsung, the walks through it are beautiful. Strybing is everybody's garden.

23

Treed at Strybing

Strybing Arboretum quite possibly has more going on in it than any other single section of the park. One of its innovations is called The Conifer Walk, a deceptively simple title for an interesting idea.

The idea is to acquaint people with the conifers, or cone-bearing trees native to California, much as the famed Alpine Garden at Schynige Platte, Switzerland, maintained by the University of Bern halfway up the Jungfrau, is arranged to acquaint visitors with the native alpine plants.

As it happens, California has fifty-four species of native conifers, a greater number than can be found in any other single state. Of this number thirteen are endemic, which merely means they are not found in other places. Thirty-nine of the natives are already growing in Strybing Arboretum and more will be added in the foreseeable future. In the past the student of botany, or visitor of inquiring mind, had to seek out the trees laboriously, comparing needles, bark, and physical conformation, never quite sure he had pinned down the Lawson cypress or the Bishop pine.

The walker who goes to Strybing Arboretum today will find the native conifers identified by a numbered stake and a label giving both the common and the Latin name. Begin this walk at the main entrance of the arboretum, just north of the Garden Center. Walk past the small planted circle to the larger oval beyond. Tree number one is a lordly Monterey pine within the oval, a little to the left. Since The Conifer Walk makes a loop and returns you to this spot, the last tree, number twenty, a noble Monterey cypress, is also nearby. Disregard it now, however, and take the walk that leads downhill behind the Garden Center. About thirty paces toward Lincoln Way, you will meet tree two, the Lawson cypress. The giant cedar follows as tree three. Tree four, the dawn redwood, is not a native now, but it

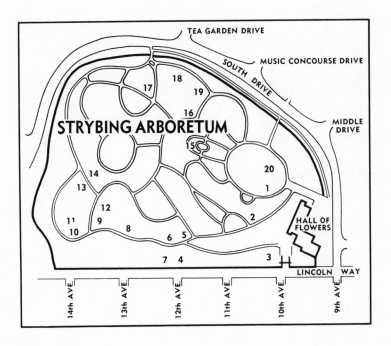

was a million years ago, and has been included because of its close resemblance to the coastal redwood. In quick succession the walker will also see a Douglas fir, a Western yew, a Western hemlock, and a California juniper.

Bear west along the path until you are abreast of the greenhouse, a gift of the Strybing Arboretum Society. Tree nine, a fine specimen of Torrey pine, is across the walk from it by the pumphouse. After tree ten, the California nutmeg, turn right. You will then be at the Redwood Trail, another unusual walk. Take the Redwood Trail to see the coastal redwood itself, tree eleven, and the beach pine, tree twelve. En route you will pass the outdoor classroom, a pleasant place to rest and sun. Here as part of an in-service training program for teachers, the idea for The Conifer Walk evolved. During the coming years, more and more San Francisco school children will find themselves using Strybing Arboretum as a living laboratory and visiting these same trees.

Tree thirteen, the incense cedar, is back on the main walk, as is tree fourteen, the giant sequoia. Tree fifteen, the Sitka spruce, requires a digression, left.

Return to the main walk and take it toward the commemorative Strybing Bench and the fountain beyond it. Tree sixteen, an atypical sprawling Bishop pine, will be found south of the bench. Take the next left to find tree seventeen, the giant fir, also known as the stinking fir because its cut wood smells so bad. The Santa Lucia fir, tree eighteen, is across the walk. Circle the pond for the ponderosa pine, tree nineteen, which stands in a clump of Woodwardia ferns. From this vantage, the fountain, Garden Center, and the end of the trail are all in plain sight.

24

Plants of the Indians at Strybing

Plants of the Indians; a Self-Guiding Nature Trail, is the title of one of several pamphlets describing walks through Strybing Arboretum, the horticulturist's corner of Golden Gate Park. Published by the Strybing Arboretum Society under a grant from the Zellerbach Family Fund, this, and the other pamphlets describing self-guiding trails (the Redwood Trail, The Conifer Walk, and the Arthur Menzies Garden of California Native Plants), are detailed enough to guide the adventurous soul who wishes to strike out on his own in the curving maze of arboretum paths.

Plants of the Indians, the all-time favorite for the greening of school children, was written and illustrated by John Kipping, the lively minded former director of education for the arboretum. This walk begins, as most arboretum walks do, at the information kiosk beside the main entrance at South Drive. If you are coming by public transportation, the 10 Monterey and 72 Haight-Sunset stop at Ninth and Lincoln Way, the N-Judah

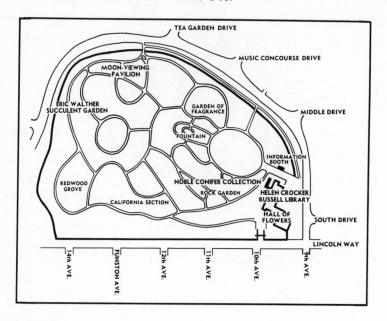

streetcar and the 6 Masonic and 66 Quintara one and two blocks away at Irving or Judah.

To seek out the unusual plants yourself, enter the arboretum through the impressive double gate, beyond the Hall of Flowers designed by Appleton and Wolford, who also designed the Marina library. Stop to pick up your pamphlet at the kiosk from smiling Laura Petri, who has served here longer than the kiosk, or from one of the other Society volunteers. If you see a group gathering there, ask which walk is being scheduled.

If not, walk through the second set of gates and bear left downhill just beyond the Helen Crocker Russell Horticultural Library, taking the left fork in the path. The route you will be following was a road that preceded the formation of Golden Gate Park. At one time it passed a little lake, which has disappeared as the water table in the city dropped with each area that has been built up. Ponds in the area are remnants of this watery past. In the Japanese garden on your right, signaled by the large stone lantern given by Mr. and Mrs. William T. Sesnon, look in the pond for plant number one, the yellow pond lily, *Nuphar polysepalum.* To us it is merely ornamental, like other plants on the trail. To the Klamath, Modoc, Quinalt, and Makah Indians, it was a staple of their diet and a medicine. Roots were baked for food, boiled for medicine; seeds were popped, ground into a sort of poi, or sometimes fermented.

Look on your left on the opposite side of the trail for plant two, a big Western red cedar, *Thuja plicata.* This was the canoe cedar or "salmon cedar" of the Northwest. Indians made dugouts, houses, totem poles, boxes, and cooking utensils from the wood; grass skirts, rope, string, mats, and capes from the bark; baskets from the roots and painkillers from the buds.

At each fork in the trail, bear left until you are in the Arthur Menzies Garden of California Native Plants, named for the long time superintendent of acquisitions at Strybing. This area contains such necessaries to the Indians as the Douglas fir, *Pseudotsuga menziesii,* named for David Douglas, who narrowly escaped a war party of eight hostile Umpqua Indians while observing the tree for the first time in 1826. Poison oak, blue elderberry, manzanita, buckeye, milkweed, pinyon, and black sage were also necessaries to the Indians.

Follow the painted four-foot wooden stakes stenciled Indian Trail to number twelve, the coast live oak, *Quercus agrifolia.* You will then be abreast of the Strybing greenhouse complex. Pause here to get your bearings. Four trails lead toward it, including the one you are on. Take the middle of three paths you face. This leads into the Redwood Trail, alongside a fine stand of scouring rush, the *Equisetum hiemale,* planted here by Art Menzies, who once taught me to file a broken fingernail with it. Cowlitz Indians ate the spore cones with salmon roe. Quileute used the boiled plants to kill head lice, but almost all tribes used the stems, whose ridges are filled with silica, to polish bows, arrows, and arrowheads.

When you have sought out plants thirteen through seventeen along the Redwood Trail, return to the greenhouses and look for the reservoir visible near a maintenance shed. Head back into the California native plant section. You will pass chaparral yucca, from which the Indians made their own yucca dew shampoo, and squaw bush, to another pond where the Indian Trail concludes with plant twenty, cattails, whose pollen is a food equal to rice and corn flour. In *Othello,* Shakespeare wrote pityingly of the "base Indian" who threw away a pearl. If he could walk the Indian Plant Trail, he might change his mind today about who has thrown away a treasure.

25

A Walk for Gardeners

In San Francisco, the walk of choice for any true gardener is in Strybing Arboretum, a series of contiguous gardens in Golden Gate Park so botanically dynamic a man could walk it daily all his life and discover something new each time.

Strybing is also so beautiful, anyone can enjoy it, whether he knows a bladdernut *(Staphlea trifolia* L.) from a nannyberry *(Vibernum lentago* L.) or a quaking aspen *(Populus tremuloides* Michx.) from any other bole in the ground.

The place to start is a few hundred feet north of the Ninth Avenue and Lincoln Way intersection where a pair of tremendous ornamental iron gates mounted in pink concrete blocks to match the Garden Center building leads into the grounds.

One of the gardens in the arboretum honors the late Junea Wangeman Kelley and is the gift of twelve of her grateful students. For forty-five years, Mrs. Kelley conducted "birders" on field trips for the University of California Extension, many through the arboretum.

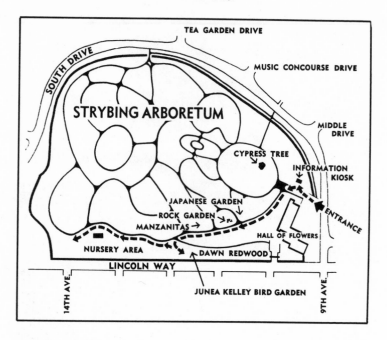

Stop at the information kiosk to buy a map. Then go through the gates and bear hard left before you reach a big circle of undulating lawn. The fountain visible beyond the biggest cypress tree in the park commemorates Helene Strybing, whose bequest made the arboretum possible. Until Robert Tetlow redesigned the great circle of lawn, it was a flat victory garden. Six feet of earth came out of the center to create this swale.

Walk downhill in a southwesterly direction, passing en route magnolias and delicate Japanese cherry trees. In the midst of the magnolias, a large stone lantern, the gift of Mr. and Mrs. William T. Sesnon, will alert the walker to a charming little Japanese garden surrounding a reflecting pond fed by waterfalls.

Walk a few more steps to come abreast of the rock garden, surrounded by the distinguished Noble collection of dwarf conifers. "If all the rare plants are not named, be patient," one supervisor pleads. "Someone regularly rapes the labels."

At the west end of the pond, bear left where the two asphalt paths intersect. Take the low road about fifty paces and bear left. Another fifty paces along, a redwood chip path enters the Junea Kelley Bird Garden. Go in to find the elbow of a meandering creek planted to attract birds. The rusty look on the Monterey cypress near Lincoln Way, by the way, is a result of "physiological stress," a phrase created by the Department of Plant Pathology at the University of California to indicate the

The Arboretum is home for many tame squirrels.

suffering plants undergo in our deteriorating environment. In a word, smog.

Notice the deciduous dawn redwood, a tree rediscovered in China in 1945. A plaque honoring Mrs. Kelley is affixed to the big rock by the two-plank bridge.

Bear right to find stepping stones over the creek and a sunny bench beside the pond. Here birders can defect to watch the hummingbirds and quail. Gardeners will want to forge onward for a look at the plantings of manzanitas in the garden of native California plants just across the way.

The civic minded will also want to take the main walk to the back end of the arboretum, to see beyond the greenhouse the new nature trail named for John Muir.

26

Suntrap in Strybing

There is a footpath in San Francisco that rambles through a laboratory, a library, and a classroom, all outdoors. The laboratory is a two-acre woodland where more than 100 plants, spanning 2 billion years of botanical evolution, live symbiotically for anyone to study or inspect.

The library consists of the plants themselves, systematically identified for those who have not learned to read trees or botanese. The classroom, however, is a real lecture hall, oval shaped and bordered with English yew hedge to make a warm suntrap. Its lectern is a redwood log on which one can count the 182 growth rings. Its benches are three-quarter logs of redwood, especially cut so the bark will not peel.

This outdoor school has been called, with commendable simplicity, the Redwood Trail. It is to be found in the southwest corner of Strybing Arboretum.

To enjoy this innovation, begin at the Garden Center, Ninth and Lincoln Way. The main gate to the arboretum, just adjacent to the building, has two matched pairs of gridwork set into concrete blocks. Go through both sets. Beyond the inner gate, bear left downhill behind the building. At each succeeding fork, hold to the path that parallels Lincoln Way.

Walking through the arboretum, like looking for a reference in an encyclopedia, offers so many enticements on the way that it takes singleness of purpose to resist digressions. This low road, especially, has many temptations, among them an Oriental garden with great stone lanterns; a rock garden planted with a collection of natural dwarf conifers and low-growing perennial flowering plants, many of them alpine; and a stream, along which grow quaking aspen and a dry arroyo.

Forebear these, if you can, and walk past the propagation greenhouse and the pumphouse. Pass the next fork. A sign next to the wood-chip trail on the right marks the beginning of the Redwood Trail. The landmark is a large stand of equisetum, or

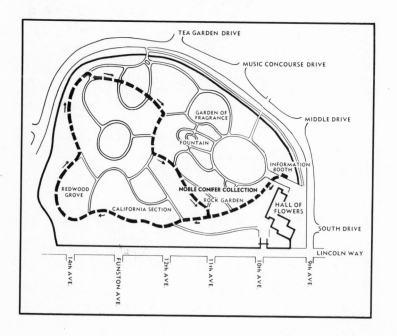

Skunk cabbage on the Redwood Trail.

horsetail reed, the "grow-it-yourself Brillo pads." Indians used it to polish arrowheads and pioneers to scour pots.

Beyond the shadowy depths of the Redwood Trail, look for a little footbridge. Across it the redwood chips of the trail wind in and out among thallophytes, bryophytes, pteridophytes, and spermatophytes. The botanical names, complex enough for graduate students, are supported by common names on the markers, together with information simple enough for school children to read.

Coastal redwoods, *Sequoia sempervirens,* planted in 1889, are the basis for this living laboratory. Ferns, azaleas, wild ginger, and other native species were planted to show the inter-dependent plant community that thrives in the moist temperate climate of the redwood belt. The walker will find the classroom, a great place to rest, about a third of the way along the trail. The trail comes out in a meadow after passing through the wilderness, a redwood forest in miniature.

27

Moon-Viewing Pavilion

"*Ten tahaku uma koyuru,*" the Japanese say traditionally in praise of autumn. "The sky is high and the horses fatten." Then, by way of thanksgiving, they prepare a little feast and floral offering to the moon, write a haiku or two in celebration of fall, or best of all, go moon-viewing. The harvest moon shines as movingly on Matsushima as it does along the Wabash or on San Francisco Bay.

It was with traditional fanfare that members of Ikebana International concluded (in October 1977) five years of effort to launch the Moon-Viewing Pavilion and Garden, their new gift to Strybing Arboretum, with a Tsuki-mi party. Tsuki-mi means—you've guessed it—moon viewing, and not what it sounds like in fractured Japanese. An altar was set up near the little pond that has been graced with a formal moon-viewing platform. On it was the classic bowl of rice dumplings, an arrangement of seven wildflowers and symbolic grasses, and one-eyed Daruma, the little roly-poly, red-clad god. Like so many other things Japanese, the bestowing of eyes on Daruma has its formalities. One is painted on when a project is begun; the other when it is completed. On this occasion, Mrs. Toshikazu Maeda, wife of the Consul General of Japan, wielded the ritual brush. Then sake, Sapporo, and Suntory flowed, baskets of viands circulated among the kimonos, politicians, and horticulturalists, the music of samisens floated over the water, and tiki torches flickered as the gentle movements of the *hanagasa odori,* or parasol dance, were reflected on the pond. It was all there but the guest of honor. The moon didn't make the scene until three hours after the viewing was over.

Which leads to a leading question of the day. Inasmuch as Golden Gate Park is closed at night, what good is a moon-viewing pavilion, pond, and garden if you can't view the moon from it? The answer is that you can. By prearrangement any large group can enjoy a moon viewing. Indeed, some groups will sponsor an annual full moon Tsuki-mi. Barring that, the moon-viewing pavilion is a pretty place to look at, and view from, in the daytime, too.

To make this walk, take the 10 Monterey bus to the Tea Garden stop (or park where you can along the South Drive). The gate is on the southwest side of the street. Walk in, bear right, not at the first asphalt walk as one is tempted to do, but at the second. This brings you part of the way around a wooded oval. At the next junction where five paths cross, take the second asphalt walk to the right a second time. This brings one past two big monkey-puzzle trees (even non-horticulturalists will know them by their puzzling twisted arms) and a dramatic mayten tree. If you don't know a mayten from a linden or a malus from a prunus, look at the base for its label. The tags give both common and Latin names. About fifty more paces brings one to the Zellerbach Garden, dedicated by Mrs. Stephen B. Coney in 1967 in honor of her grandmother. Go up its loop of flagstone walk to discover a pleasant, sheltered bench and stone table. Then return to the asphalt walk and continue to the right. The

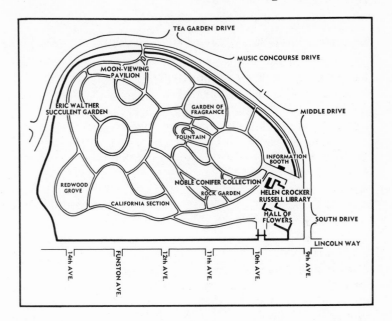

moon-viewing garden, designed by Henry Matsutani of Concord, is the very next one, distinguished by a pond, well-placed rocks, resident ducks, tremendous trees, and a woodland trail that leads to the platform on the water. Go out on it for a view across the lawn to see how the moon must rise with Buena Vista hill in the distance, framed by foliage. The tree sheltering the platform, by the way, is a rare coriaria.

When the moon-viewing garden has revealed its charms, continue around bearing consistently right to locate two more gardens. One is the Arthur Menzies native plant garden honoring the late, much loved superintendent of the arboretum. Across the walk from it fifty paces farther is the Opera Garden, donated by Friends of Golden Gate Park, which ultimately will contain all the plants mentioned in operas. Bearing left creates a loop, finally crossing the little footbridge to return to the Tea

Garden entrance. If the peaceful gardens haven't inspired you to compose a suitable autumn haiku as you stroll, consider this one by Soseki:

The winds that blow
Ask them which leaf of the tree
Will be next to go.

28

Heidelberg Hill

On the first Sunday after the first full moon to follow the vernal equinox, whatever your religion, if you are mortal, there's a primordial stirring in the blood. It's the annual surge of hope and renewal. The country man gets hints of it wherever he turns, but for the San Franciscan, the best place to enjoy it is in Golden Gate Park.

There is a fine vantage point from which to watch spring abloom in Strybing Arboretum. It has been cleverly situated on Heidelberg Hill, a wooded knoll about fifty feet high that overlooks the Strybing Memorial Fountain, a grassy oval of lawn, the Duck Pond, and what used to be known as "The Panel." Since any elevation, however slight, opens new vistas, this is well worth the visit, especially when the arboretum's fine collection of crab apple trees is in bloom. En route to it, one also passes the little-known Biblical Garden that features plants of the Old Testament.

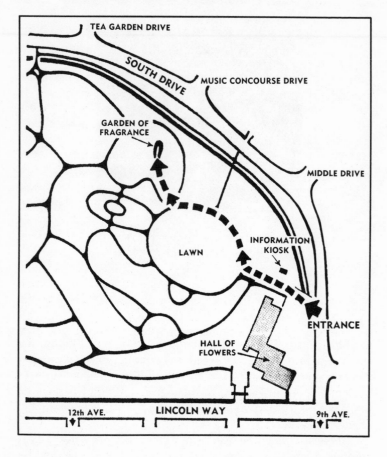

To do this walk, transport yourself, preferably by public transporation (Muni buses 10, 71, and 72 stop here), to Ninth Avenue and Lincoln Way. Walk past the pink Garden Center building designed by architects Appleton and Wolford, to the ornamental gates just north of the building. Go in. In a few steps you will be abreast of the kiosk maintained by the Strybing Arboretum Society. Collectors line up at the gate when the society sponsors its annual plant sale, eager to snap up rarities unavailable elsewhere. Stop for a map or pamphlet if you wish, then continue through the second set of gates parallel to the Helen Crocker Russell Horticultural Library.

Once through the second gate, bear right and follow the curving walkway around the oval of lawn. When you reach the first right turn, pause at this serene corner for a moment. Try to envision a diamond-stack locomotive on a Southern Pacific Railroad track coming right along this way in front of you. During the California Midwinter International Exposition of 1894, this was the *Deutsches Dorf,* or German Village, stop on a Southern Pacific spur track run into the park from the Park Street & Ocean Railroad line along Lincoln Way. In a few hundred feet from this spot, it fanned out into eight additional tracks. One led to what is now the Garden of Shakespeare's Flowers, but was then the Chinese Village, another to the Mechanical Arts Building that stood where the Academy of Sciences is located. A third approached Agricultural Hall, now site of the M. H. de Young Memorial Museum. The other five went into a tremendous railroad exhibit located farther along within the arboretum.

Continue on to the second right and turn with it. In a trice you are at another path that goes off to the left between parallel stone walls. Left of the nearer half circle of wall is the Garden of Fragrance for the blind. A series of plants selected for their subtle scents and sensuous foliage are grown in raised beds and labeled in Braille. It is one of three gardens stipulated in the will of the late Helene Strybing. To the right, following the outer curve of wall, is the collection of plants from the Pentateuch given by ladies of Congregation Emanu-El on their 125th anniversary. Song of Solomon 6:11 is quoted in their dedicatory booklet: "I went down into the garden of nuts to look at the green plants of the valley to see whether the vine budded, and the pomegranates were in flower." Both pomegranate and grapevine are among the plants along the wall and had budded. But I looked in vain for an almond tree or two among the trees in the fronting lawn.

When you pass the new commemorative bench, look twenty feet beyond on your left for a beautiful broad staircase

made of railroad ties and brush chips. It meanders uphill gracefully through fine old magnolias and rhododendrons. This is the
path up Heidelberg Hill. If you had been here in 1894, it would
also have been the site of a replica of *Schlöss Heidelberg,* or
Heidelberg Castle, and a Schwarzwald *bierstube* and restau-

Herbs that are nice to touch and smell grow by the wall.

rant, called appropriately *Zum Goldenen Bar,* the Golden Bear Inn. It was one of the hits of "Sunset City," as this part of the exposition was known. Anyone who ever sat inside the board-room at Whitney's Playland at the Beach, as I did, can boast of having been within the walls of this long vanished inn, for that's where the ornate paneling went—after the ball was over.

Climb the steps to discover at their crest a broad open area, set about with benches, that looks through daylighted old trees over the lively scene below. Crab apples and the Strybing foun-tain animate the foreground. The intrusive towers to the south-east belong to the University of California Medical Center. View-ers in the past who looked in that direction from Heidelberg Castle saw instead its predecessor, the Affiliated Colleges, out-lined against Mount Sutro.

When you have surveyed the view to your heart's content, stroll down Heidelberg Hill again and bear left to discover some of the finest old rhododendrons and camellias in the park. Curve around the hill with the main walkway bearing consis-tently left until you are in sight of the Duck Pond, then walk toward it and cross the bridge. In mating season, the cacophony is better than a sign and will lead you to it. Once across the bridge you are almost at the South Drive entrance across from the Tea Garden. If the arboretum's sweet serenity seems more enchanting, bear right shy of the gate and you will come alongside a quiet stream and marsh. Back at the foot of Heidelberg Hill bear right toward the landmark fountain and the broad oval of lawn, then left to return to the main entrance.

29

Wonderful Place to Walk

"Water seems to have a fascination for everybody," said the Municipal Report of 1893 in its description of the then newly completed Stow Lake.

Now, today, Stow Lake is still a fascinator, rippling and restful. It was around the lake, one of the pleasantest loops in the city, that visitors to the Midwinter Fair of 1894 went for romance.

To make this walk, begin at the boathouse, no longer very rustic, just south of John F. Kennedy Drive and almost opposite Seventeenth Avenue. Walk around to the front to find the boat rental concession and snack bar. The original concessionaire was granted the first permit allowing an automobile to come into the park. The permit was issued in 1901 to allow him to transport food.

No one then could envision the traffic jams of cars that were to follow in his tire tracks.

Go to the water's edge and bear right on the macadam walk, originally a carriageway, that encircles the lake. Notice the several islands, ideal for duck nests, in the water. The largest is Strawberry Hill, elevation 414 feet, the highest point in the park and named for the wild strawberries once found on its sides. It existed before the park as southern high point of the long transverse ridge that dissects the area somewhat diagonally from southeast to northwest.

Stow Lake, in contrast, is totally artificial, made on a base of puddled clay hauled from a quarry that once stood at Turk

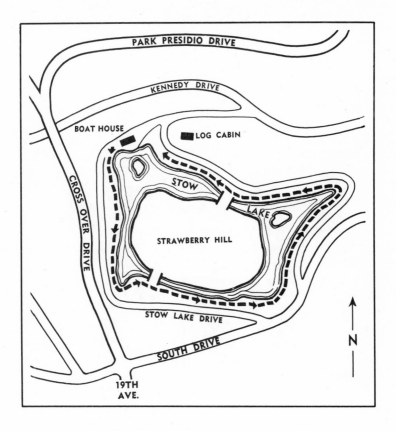

and Divisadero streets. Crushed rock tops the clay under about three and a half feet or 15,331,700 gallons of water. Credit for the lake usually goes to one-time Park Commissioner W. W. Stow.

It might as reasonably have been named Prichard Lake. Captain Prichard, who served under Stonewall Jackson and led his company during Pickett's Charge at Gettysburg, was park superintendent from 1876 to 1881. It was he who drew up the plans for a reservoir on Strawberry Hill and for an overflow lake below.

As you walk, look west to see how the slight elevation safely separates pedestrians from the traffic. During the Midwinter Fair of 1894 and for twelve years after, the great romantic ride on which to take your lady was by horse-drawn hack around the lake, then up to Sweeny Observatory on Strawberry Hill.

The rustic bridge on the left was reserved in those days, as

The Sweeny Observatory, before its destruction in the 1906 earthquake.

now, for pedestrians. As enticing as it seems, continue around the lake for the nonce, looking through the trees for unexpected glimpses of the University of California Medical School. When you reach a view bench looking at the lake, sit a moment.

Until 1962, when storm damage collapsed the understructure, Huntington Falls, one of our noted tourist attractions, cascaded in two exciting leaps 110 feet down Strawberry Hill from the reservoirs above, a necessary and much-loved part of Golden Gate Park's thrifty reclamation system. Funds are now available to reconstruct the falls.

The Roman Bridge is where carriages once went up. The agile may want to cross here and climb the hill to seek out what few remains are left of Sweeny Observatory, the park's main casualty of the 1906 earthquake.

Those who prefer a level walk can bear right along the road and soon reach the Pioneer Log Cabin. It stands here thanks to the courtliness of P. J. "White Hat" McCarthy, once mayor of San Francisco. After the 1906 earthquake had destroyed Pioneer Hall on Fourth Street, the Association of Pioneer Women of California held their monthly meetings as picnics in the park.

Mayor McCarthy, astride his horse, espied them one day, was concerned over what women of such refinement would do when the rains came, and gallantly arranged to have the cabin placed here. It was completed in 1911 and enlarged in 1932.

30

Walk Up Strawberry Hill

Some one of these days a hip young composer will rejuvenate musical comedy with a bright new offering. The setting will be Golden Gate Park. When Huntington Falls is restored, complete with stepping stones at the foot of the cascade, the whole opus could take place on Strawberry Hill in Stow Lake.

For those newcomers to San Francisco, Huntington Falls was once our most beautiful unnatural phenomenon. Between 1892 and 1962, it tumbled, first in rapids, then in two tall cascades, seventy-five feet down Strawberry Hill over a picturesque backdrop of rocks and ferns and under footbridges to meet Stow Lake at its base.

Every accordion fold of "Scenic San Francisco" postcards during that time included at least one view of it. It was not only tantalizing to see, and symbolic of eternal youth as its waters came flashing down, but thrifty as well.

The aeration was part of the water reclamation system used to irrigate the whole park. If you climb to the top of Strawberry

Hill, at 425 feet above sea level the highest point in the park, the vestiges are still visible.

So are some of the red remains of Sweeny Observatory, a two-story amphitheaterlike building big enough for horses and carriages to turn around in. It was once built on the crest of Strawberry by the man who gave telegraph service to the Western world.

To make this walk, transport yourself to Stow Lake, between Kennedy Drive and South Drive near Nineteenth Avenue. Cross via either the Rustic Bridge or the Roman Bridge and follow the broad trail around the base of the island, rising

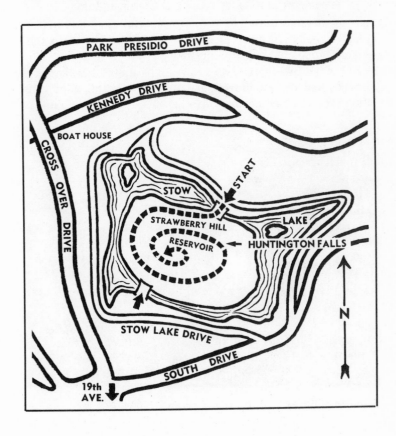

with it. Since there is nowhere to go but up, you can't get lost for long on Strawberry. There is a choice of trails, but the broadest, long ago used for sightseeing carriages, is the easiest.

Not long ago I made this walk with one of Golden Gate Park's most dedicated buffs. She reminded me, documenting her words with early maps and annual reports from her own collection, that there had been two footbridges across the Huntington stream, one in concrete that imitated bent boughs of wood.

We explored what was left of the foundation of the falls, although I don't recommend this for the average walker, and discovered that the deepest stone work, probably the one that railroad magnate Collis P. Huntington, who gave $25,000 to create the falls, enjoyed, seemed to be overlain by three subsequent repairs in poured concrete.

At about two-thirds of the way up the trail, the walker will discover that one of the original reservoirs is still filled. The other, source of the cataract, can be traced out on the crest of

From Strawberry Hill the vistas open in all directions.

the hill. It made a reflecting pond for Sweeny Observatory, until the 1906 quake that toppled the Romanesque building. Maybe someday water will again rush down the watercourse at the rate of 1.6 million gallons a day to keep the park green and glistening.

From the top of Strawberry Hill, the Farallones are visible, a little north by west, with the Cliff House in the foreground. Mount Tamalpais, the Golden Gate Bridge, Fort Point, and Mountain Lake can all be discerned through the trees. When the air has been cleaned by an on-shore breeze, Mount Diablo stands out clearly.

Whether the *fraises de bois*, which gave Strawberry Hill its name, still grow wild on its steep slopes, only the elves know.

31

Visit the Other Panhandle

Section thirteen of Golden Gate Park is the handsomely planted twenty-three acres whose distance, unlike the rest of the park, is greater from north to south than it is from east to west.

If you are tempted to say there is no such place, come some fair day for a walk along the Presidio Parkway, or as it was called on the E.C.D. Price and Company city map of 1910, "the Presidio and Park Panhandle." Today it is better known as Park Presidio Boulevard. It's still part of Golden Gate Park.

Begin this walk at the corner of Funston and Fulton, across from that section of the park which contains Heroes' Grove and the Rose Garden. Cross Funston Avenue. Immediately you are at the perimeter sidewalk of the parkway, "seven blocks of land, each block 600 feet long and 240 feet wide" according to an early park commissioners' report, "nearly one mile extending from the northern boundary line of Golden Gate Park to the south line of the military reservation at a point not far from the old U.S. Marine Hospital." When the land was purchased, in

1903, at the now unbelievably low price of $360,000, park commissioners happily predicted, "The new boulevard running through the main body of the Richmond District from Golden Gate Park to the Presidio will open up a new field of park life."

It also opened up a desirable place to live, as a glance north along the affluent row of homes that front on Funston, shielded from traffic noises and exhausts by the great shade trees growing on a raised berm, confirms.

Walk twenty feet farther west and look north again to see a growth of lawn, struggling to obscure the red-rock bridle path that meanders gracefully through the east side of the park. Originally much used by horsemen, who can no longer get across Fulton Street, it now makes a great promenade for walkers. Fol-

Presidio Parkway shelters fine old homes.

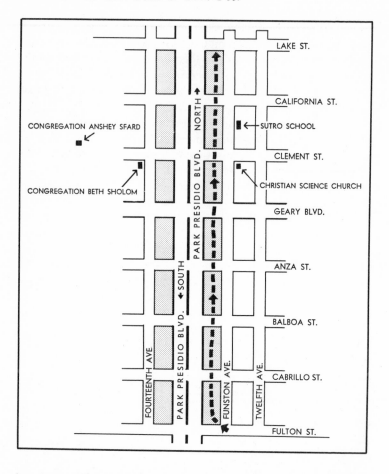

low it toward Mountain Lake, the Richmond District's great historic prize. Down through the years, more than one young horseman must have pretended to be Juan Bautista de Anza riding toward a night's encampment on the shores of Mountain Lake.

As you walk, it becomes apparent that the shade trees are planted in groups, with here a grove of gnarled "tea trees," like frozen dinosaurs, there a stand of "manna gums," like maidens drying long tresses in the wind, interspersed with stalwart soldierlike pines. Many are varieties first tested for San Francisco weather in the slightly wider Baker to Stanyan Street Panhandle. Since the microclimate of the Presidio Parkway varies from one side of the street to the other, its plantings were designed to thrive within the variations.

As you walk, look for glimpses of Sutro School, for the familiar columns of a classic Christian Science church, and for the striking columns of Congregation Beth Sholom on the west side of Clement and Fourteenth. If it is an average day, the walker will have to detour to stoplights at corners (especially on the major shopping streets, California, Geary, and Clement) in order to cross.

Already eroded twice down through the years by expanding auto lanes to serve non-resident motorists, the parkway, once a model for planners in how to handle traffic without destroying a neighborhood, is once again under the curse of the cars. If you had always intended to stroll this graceful esplanade, don't wait too long.

32

To the Source of Rainbow Falls

The casual walker who comes along John F. Kennedy Drive in Golden Gate Park will discern the happy burble of falling water in the region parallel to Twentieth Avenue. What he hears is Rainbow Falls.

As any child can demonstrate, there is some primal urge within us all to seek the source of running water and, if possible, to track it to its ultimate destination. It was a great search for a lost river that prompted Congress to authorize in 1842 the expeditions to the Far West of Captain J. C. Fremont, paleontologist John Hull, and botanist John Torrey.

Tracking Rainbow Falls is easier, the matter of a pleasant hour. Enter the park at Fulton Street and Park Presidio Boulevard, cutting through the meadow to John F. Kennedy Drive. At John F. Kennedy Drive, walk west until the rush, splash, and gurgle of leaping water drowns out the traffic noises from Crossover Bridge, overhead.

Near its base is a pond filled by the cascade that leaps over the cliffside above. Trees, shrubs, and rushes surround it, sometimes sheltering nesting mallards. Look carefully at the cliff. These red rocks of the Franciscan formation belong to the Jurassic period, more than a hundred million years old, and in them hide the radiolaria, the oldest fossils in the Bay Area. In the Division of Mines *Geologic Guidebook to the Bay Area,* Dr. Leo Hertlein of the Academy of Sciences recommends this cliff as one of the best outcroppings for paleontologic examination.

Don't expect to see the fossils with the bare eye. But a little close scrutiny will reveal artificial grotto work and electric light sockets. When the falls were installed originally in the early 1930s, a world still enraptured by the spell of Thomas A. Edison marveled at the rainbows the spray created around each lighted bulb—hence the name of Rainbow Falls.

To reach the source, take the path labeled Prayer Book Cross just east of the pond. Less than fifty feet uphill, the water rushes out of the ground, piped from the reservoir on nearby

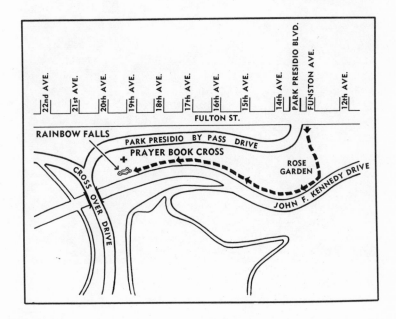

This is the captain of the pond.

Strawberry Hill in the center of Stow Lake. Fencing prevents kayakers from shooting these rapids. Retrace your steps to the pond once you have examined the cairn from which the water comes. At the western end, a brook takes off, passing a small cave that has a watery floor and was once lighted, like the falls.

The brook, like the walk and John F. Kennedy Drive, all go under the bridge through a garden of stone. In a few minutes it divides, as natural rivers do, and rejoins its main stream a little farther along. Finally, its course broadens into a delta, flowing through and around stepping stones at the mouth of Lloyd Lake. Alan Fleischhacker recalled playing on the stepping stones as a boy, as children do today. His parents, Mr. and Mrs. Herbert Fleischhacker, were the donors of this lighthearted ornament to the park.

If you really want to trace Rainbow Falls to its source, you must go all the way to France. "I think it was in 1924 that my parents made the trip to Paris that inspired this gift," Mr. Fleischhacker told me. "There was a falls like it in the Bois de Boulogne. They fell in love with it and brought back pictures. John McLaren put a man to copying it, and Rainbow Falls is the result."

33

The Path to Prayer Book Cross

A rune is a secret, a whisper, a letter. There is mystery in a rune, and poetry, and the runic cross in Golden Gate Park is true to its Celtic origins. Come seek me out! The magic mark in the sky not far from Nineteenth Avenue and Fulton Street seems to beckon when glimpsed distantly through trees from unexpected places. Come to me and I will reveal hidden pools, forgotten flutes, and possibly dryads and druids.

Elusive as a dryad, this fifty-seven foot sandstone symbol of an ancient form of punishment has a way of disappearing. The closer one gets to the cross, the harder it is to find. Many paths that seem to lead to it go somewhere else. This enhances its mystery, of course. Concealment is the essence of secrets.

The path that actually goes up the little eminence on which it stands hasn't been on city or park maps for many years. It begins at Fulton Street, hard by Park Presidio Boulevard, a chute that has created through the park a three-block-wide swath of dead "buffer space" almost useless for recreation. If you can endure the drive for one walk, stroll into the park on the east side of it.

On your left, the cool greenery of Heroes' Grove makes a backdrop for the fragile loveliness of the Rose Garden, one of the few places in the park where the climate is the optimum for rosarians. Ignore for now the walkway through it that leads to John F. Kennedy Drive and take the westering path that leads to the Native Sons and Daughters Redwood Memorial Grove.

Soon the path seems to become a faint tracery of red rock in the grass as it goes upward mounting the knoll on which the cross stands. In Iona, Scotland, the ancient runic crosses that gave the designer, Ernest Coxhead, his inspiration for this one, were decked with mistletoe. This one is inscribed, instead, with the message that it is a memorial to the prayer service that Chaplain Francis Fletcher held gratefully on St. John Baptist's

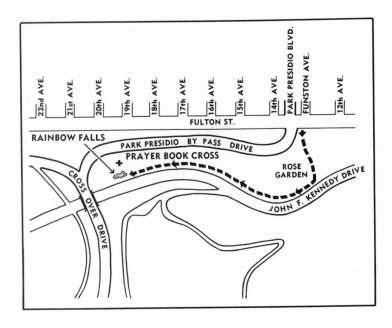

Ten thousand came here to pray every year.

Day, June 24, 1579, when Sir Francis Drake's ship, the *Golden Hinde,* put safely into what most experts believe is now Drake's Bay.

Father Fletcher's service on the shore was the first to use the English *Book of Common Prayer,* handbook of the Anglican Church, in North America. Indians prostrated themselves in pagan rites, regarding the Englishmen as gods, and Drake sailed back with the Indians' scepter of sovereignty, a feather mantle, after posting his brass plate proclaiming Nova Albion.

The donor of the Prayer Book Cross, as it is nicknamed, was a Philadelphia editor and philanthropist, George W. Childs, whose $10,000 gift to San Francisco was unveiled on the opening day of the Midwinter Exposition, January 1, 1894. Thereafter, as many as 10,000 Episcopalians and Anglicans (who use the *Book of Common Prayer* to this day) made annual pilgrimages to the cross for services interrupted only by travel curtailments during the two World Wars.

"Soli Deo sit semper gloria" is the message on the cross.

There are no druids on the grass, alas, but the walker will find the rune has a secret after all. Near the base is the cairn from which Rainbow Falls, one of the more lighthearted ornaments of the park, springs gurgling down the hillside.

34

A Voyage to Yesterday

Since 1909, the most photographed landmark in Golden Gate Park has been The Portals of the Past, a romantic sextet of white marble columns that reflect themselves nicely in Lloyd Lake on any reasonably calm day.

Like flute music, this doorway has an elusive evocative quality. The walker who sits quietly looking at The Portals of the Past for any length of time will find a delicious melancholy descending on him. In old San Franciscans, this sweet sadness is tied to the lavish champagne age that preceded the 1906 earthquake and fire.

The stone frame was the portico of the A.N. Towne residence on Nob Hill and was given to the park by Clinton E. Worden. As one contemporary writer said, "It was all that was left standing on the hill after the 1906 catastrophe. Through it could be seen a city, or rather a city that had been, smoldering in ruins. The brave souls of that day summed up the civic spirit:

"This is the portal of the past—from now on, once more, forward!"

History buffs can find a photograph of the portal still in place on Nob Hill with the ruined downtown spires behind it facing page 50 in Helen Throop Purdy's *San Francisco As It Was • As It Is • And How to See It* published by Paul Elder in 1912.

To enjoy the mood, one need not know any of the history. Architects will recognize that this park ornament, however accidentally, is a successful and classic *folly* in the best sense of the word. According to Barbara Jones, author of *Follies and Grottoes,* a critique of several hundred such structures in En-

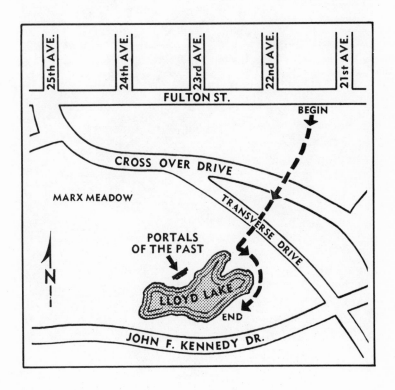

Go 'round the pond and find the marker under foot.

gland, "More mood and emotion are built into follies than into any other kind of architecture. . . . While normally emotion in architecture is expressed professionally only in a very distilled and controlled way, and then only upon a framework of logic and mathematics, the folly evokes the spectator's emotions with uncivilized directness, by stating its own and nothing else."

As John McLaren must have understood the minute he saw it, with or without its trial by fire, the graceful doorway mirrored in a lake would bring on a throat-tightening attack of *tristesse* whenever a responsive soul came upon it. And we are all responsive.

So make this walk in the sentimental spirit of its period. Bring a copy of the poems of Tennyson or Swinburne or if you're younger, Tolkien. A wicker picnic hamper stocked with a cold bird and bottle would have the essence of suitable elegance. A very imaginative man could carry the whole expedition off with nothing but a gold-headed walking stick. Be prepared to sigh a little.

Start this walk at Fulton Street 'twixt Twenty-first and Twenty-second Avenue. Soon your progress will be interrupted by Crossover Drive. Persevere and continue, crossing Transverse Drive. You arrive at Marx Meadow's eastern end. Follow Transverse Drive southeasterly for a hundred yards to reach the walk that encircles Lloyd Lake. Take it. For the best aspect of the portals, viewed across the water, bear left at the next fork.

If the silence, more musical than any song, takes you utterly into its spell, try a verse from Christina Rossetti for antidote: "When I am dead, my dearest, sing no sad songs for me," for example. That's how the Pre-Raphaelite poets endured the sweet pain of it all.

35

Roses and Windmills

The ingredients of a good walk include variety. George Macaulay Trevelyan, who claimed he had two doctors, his left leg and his right, felt that variety could best be obtained "by losing the way—a half-conscious process, which in a sense can no more be done of deliberate purpose than falling in love." And yet, he suggested, "a man can sometimes very wisely let himself drift, either into love, or into the wrong path when walking."

San Francisco has a walk for the Trevelyans of our time whose variety includes a rose garden and an opportunity to lose one's way and to find it again in a symphony of tulips, windmills, and waves.

The Golden Gate Park Rose Garden is an excellent place to begin this ramble. It is located at Funston and Fulton on the east side of the Park Presidio shortcut. In 1961 the San Francisco chapter of the American Rose Society chose this new site as suitable for testing roses in the city. Now there are sixty-three rose beds, all planted with trial varieties supplied by commercial growers and maintained by local rosarians.

The rose fanciers often at work here will bend any willing ear with the merits of Tropicana, a coral-orange hybrid tea rose, or point out an unusual sport polyandra, a weeping Margot Koster trained on a standard.

When the Rose Garden has given up its secrets, follow the path along the throughway to the Native Sons and Daughters Redwood Memorial Grove, a welcome oasis of relative quiet. Near Seventeenth Avenue, a walk cuts through to Kennedy Drive. Follow it or bear uphill through the woodland path. Either way leads in time to Prayer Book Cross on the cliff above Rainbow Falls.

In John McLaren's day, this was a peaceful spot, suitable for soul-searching. After investigation, the walker will soon shun it for quieter parts of the park. Many are to be found west of the Nineteenth Avenue cutoff.

Follow Kennedy Drive under the bridge near Rainbow

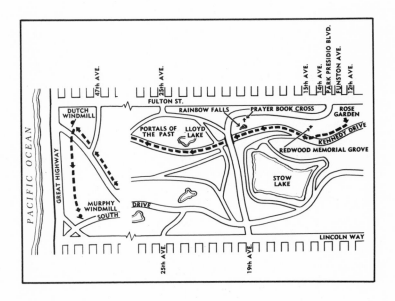

Falls, past Lloyd Lake and The Portals of the Past. Then if "getting lost" seems an amusing idea, here is a maze in which to do it. The roads and choices are many. By bearing north, in time the walker will reach a dirt road, seldom used. Take it, or any path you cross leading west.

Ultimately you will reach the Queen Wilhelmina Garden, named in 1962 as a tribute to the late queen of the Netherlands. It surrounds a tall landmark, the old North Mill, a Dutch windmill with tulips around it, such as a visitor to Holland might find adjacent to similar mills in the Netherlands in the spring of the year.

Just beyond it is an old railbed that leads to its counterpart, Murphy's Mill, at the south end of the park. Or if waves seem more inviting, cross Great Highway and you are at Ocean Beach.

36

Three Little Lakes

It is fun sometimes to pick out a part of the park that is not a regular haunt, that you may have only driven past. There is scenic magic, for example, well off the tourist trail in the area surrounding Metson, Mallard, and Elk Glen Lakes.

To make this walk, go into the park from Lincoln Way at Thirty-fourth Avenue, via the path that crosses the bridle path and South Drive to reach Middle Drive abreast of the polo field. Bear east alongside of Middle Drive following the left fork of the road. Soon you will reach a lovely sheet of water in an Oriental setting that almost looks like a mountain lake that may overflow the road. This is Metson Lake, man made, about three feet deep, and named for William H. Metson, a park commissioner at the time of the 1906 earthquake. Its elevation is 173 feet above sea level, about 11 feet lower than the land was when William Hammond Hall made his original topographic survey in 1870.

At the water's edge, turn right and walk halfway around the lake until you reach a path on the south side that wanders away from the mossy banks and rock work through a grassy dell and picnic ground. Bearing southeasterly on it, one crosses a service road that gives one the feeling of being in the country. Soon one glimpses another lake, just bordering South Drive, like a geographical echo of Metson Lake.

Cross South Drive and you are on the shore of Mallard Lake, the smallest of the three in this area and named for the showy ducks that stop here on their annual migrations. For years this was known as Hobo Lake. Transient knights of the road who flocked to San Francisco to work on the Midwinter Fair often rested here between labors. Sea grass then comprised the only greenery.

Mallard Lake has nesting residents all year 'round.

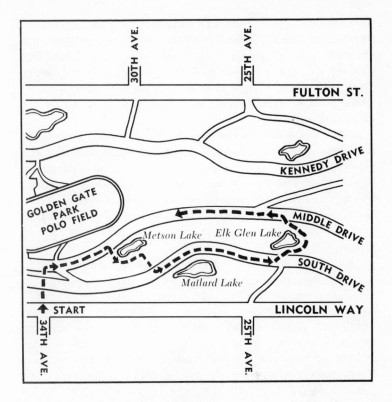

Unlike Metson Lake, Mallard Lake was a natural freshwater pond, 128 feet above sea level when this part of the park was sand dunes. The average depth is three feet two inches and the capacity is 1,436,000 gallons.

When you have rested awhile on its shore, follow the walk bordering South Drive as it meanders east. After passing a fine old grove of tree ferns and the Twenty-fifth Avenue entrance of the road, Elk Glen Lake, the largest of the three at 2,064,000 gallons, will become visible.

The elk for which this glen was named began with a gift of a mature pair of wapiti, or Roosevelt elk, from Alvinza Hayward in 1890, although wild elk may have drunk from a pond that sometimes filled this gully before it was a park. The Hayward elk thrived and multiplied until Golden Gate Park was known for its gang of elk. "This is not surprising," said the report of the park commissioners for 1912, "when it is considered that Colonel J. C. Fremont, Kit Carson, General Vallejo, Colonel Yount and others who traveled through the mountains and valleys of California from 1830 until 1850 saw countless bands of elk and deer.

"Many parks in other sections of California and some of the U.S. Reservations have been supplied with elk from the band in Golden Gate Park, and the Commissioners are now taking care of forty-four elk, twelve bucks, twenty-eight does and four fawns." There were also dwarf elk, mule deer, axis deer, black-tailed deer, moose, kangaroos, antelope, bears, bison, and peacocks in the park at that time. Most were moved to the zoo around 1935.

The sharp-eyed may catch a glimpse of quail that breed near the sewage treatment plant above the northwest corner of Elk Glen Lake. The chemist whose special charge is the park's thrifty water reclamation system (and who leads tours of the installation given advance notice) told me, "Once we had peacocks here, but the poor animals were stalked for their tail feathers by hippies and a few of them wound up barbecued by them, too. We're hoping there are enough left to repopulate the area."

Walk uphill on the north side of the lake to reach Middle Drive, then west along the walk on its south side to complete the loop back to Metson Lake. Fans of sculptor Beniamino Bufano may want to stop at the treatment plant for a look at his *Boy on a Dolphin*, now located here.

37

England in the Park

There is an aura of empire over the central part of Golden Gate Park. You feel it in the flourish of a silver-thin fishing line over the water. You hear it in the hoofbeats on the polo field. You sense it when soccer, cricket, or rugby is on the green.

For here, along about Thirty-fourth Avenue, is a thirty-acre area devoted to that heritage of games chosen because they lead a man into a merry spirit and "pleasure without any repentance afterwards," as Dame Juliana Berners described "good sports and honorable pastimes."

England's not so far away on a Sunday afternoon in the park, especially near the stadium, the stables, the Angler's Lodge, and the casting ponds. The flavor is at its fullest about 2:00 P.M. when there's soccer and rugby in progress.

To find it, begin this walk at Thirty-fourth Avenue and Lincoln Way. Walk north into the park through a shady grove of pines. At the South Drive cross the little footbridge and continue through a eucalyptus grove (watch for nettles on the right).

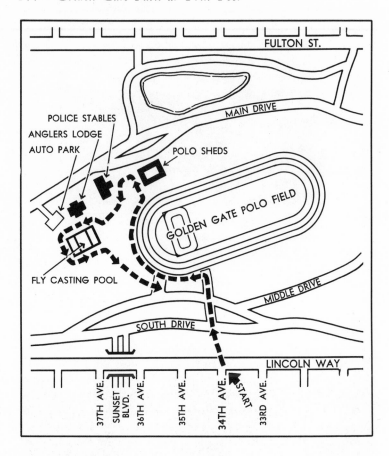

Cross Middle Drive and go through the cypress to the tunnel visible ahead. There, about the distance of a city block from Lincoln Way, is the polo stadium.

Go past a locker room through the tunnel, the southernmost of two both twenty feet wide and ten feet high, which go under a trotting track to give access to the stadium. Dead ahead will be a waist-high, chain-link fence.

On either hand will be bleachers to watch the daring game named for a pulu, or willow ball in the Balti dialect of the Indus

Valley of India. Like the course of empire, polo made its way west with the help of British cavalrymen.

Sloping toward the center of the oval fields is a grassy terrace, ten feet high and thirty feet wide, and a two-third mile bicycle track encircling it. On the rim of the bowl is a six-furlong track used for sulky racing in 1907 when the stadium was new.

Inside the bicycle track at the western end is a 220-yard cinder track and a circular quarter-mile cinder track with space inside for broad jumping, pole vaulting, and comparable exertions. The park commissioners' report of 1910 says, "Space is also given for one basketball court and six football fields. For example, Berkeley, Stanford, Yale, Harvard, Princeton and Pennsylvania could contend simultaneously for football supremacy, each with a rival team."

This six-ring circus was never held here, but the men at the police stables immediately northwest of the stadium can recall seeing a lacrosse, rugby, cricket, and football game going on simultaneously.

Fly casting pools west of the Polo Grounds.

Walk west around the oval on the trotting track toward the odd little octagon building. This is a judges' stand, the gift of Frank C. Burke, Esq. Bleachers near it are no longer in use, except for an occasional sunbather. Stables underneath and others nearby are occupied by horses for hire.

Walk toward the building with the weathervane to see the police stables.

To find Angler's Lodge, a clubhouse, and the three unusual ponds used by fly and bait casters, take the second path leading southwest down from the stadium rim. (Surf casters sometimes practice in the stadium, too, when it isn't booked for games.) At any waking hour, some devotee of angling can be found here, practicing. Skirt the ponds to find just south of them a path that gives on part of old Speedway Meadow, planted with victory gardens during World War II. A path at the east end leads up a red-rock road to the perimeter of the stadium and will return the walker to the bleachers or the Thirty-fourth Avenue shortcut.

38

Time and Shadows

There is a semisylvan path in Golden Gate Park between Lindley Meadow and Speedway Meadow that meanders through time and through a eucalyptus grove. Birds nest here and sing. Ground squirrels flick and scurry. The sunlight filters through the leaves. The setting could be *A Midsummer Night's Dream*.

It lies between the northeast end of the Polo Field and Broom Point. It can be reached by entering the park at Thirtieth Avenue and Fulton and walking south to Kennedy Drive where it borders Lindley Meadow.

Park maps should label the area "ideal picnic spots." If you would explore it, bring your friend, family picnic basket, favorite tatami mat, or Indian blanket to the upper road that rings the Polo Field. Usually there is fair parking here. Go through any of the main openings in the outer hedge and walk right, or east, away from the stables.

Within a few steps away from the berm of earth surrounding the stadium, you are in the woody swale. Usually you'll

Totem pole at Lindley Meadow.

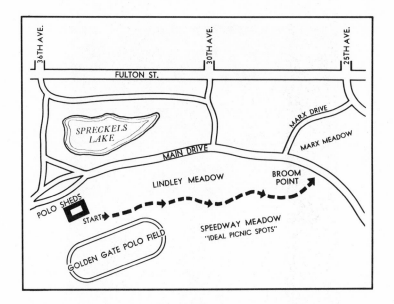

find a student reading, a pair of lovers idling in the sunshine, and the shouts of frisbee players in the distance.

It was along this section that John McLaren, among others, reputedly saw the ghostly girl in purple who would be standing forlornly at the roadside at dusk. If a gallant gentleman gave her a ride in his carriage, she would have disappeared before he reached darkness or the edge of the park.

Pause a minute when you go along this path. Stop in the vicinity of Thirtieth Avenue and look about. If you step off the path on the uphill side, you can discover in Lindley Meadow the *Goddess of the Forest,* sculptured by Dudley C. Carter and given to the city by the Golden Gate International Exposition.

Return to the path, look south instead, and try to envision the victory gardens in Speedway Meadow where San Franciscans tilled the soil to grow patriotic food during World War II. At the eastern end now there is an untilled baseball diamond.

At Broom Point, the path is interrupted across from Marx Meadow by John F. Kennedy Drive. Walking it, maybe you'll conjure up McLaren's girl in purple.

39

The Park's Tiny Ocean

For the walker who strolls around Spreckels Lake on a weekend, the fantasy that San Francisco is populated by an affluent and intelligent race of six-inch people would be easy to sustain. Racing vessels under sail, steam, gas, and electric power, all built to a storybook scale, make a recurring regatta here.

To enjoy this activity on Spreckels Lake, begin your walk at Thirty-sixth Avenue and Fulton Street. Go between 10:00 A.M. and 1:00 P.M. if you are enthusiastic about "stink pots," as power boats are fondly known in the yachting circles. If it is the stately lines of sailing craft tacking that interest you, make the trip from 1:00 P.M. till dusk.

Power prevails in the morning by agreement of members within the San Francisco Model Yacht Club. Canvas rules this little sea in the afternoon when the trade winds come up, more welcome here than they are in some parts of San Francisco.

Cross Fulton into the park and immediately at your left

hand is seven-acre Spreckels Lake, the gift of A. B. Spreckels at the time he was president of the park commission.

At the water's edge, walk east, paralleling Fulton. Before the yachtsmen have come out to play, wild fowl paddle and feed here. Duck down often floats on the water giving the surface an odd flatness.

As you walk around the lakelet, an old gentleman on a shiny bicycle, bevies of small children, senior citizens en route to a nearby center, strolling lovers, and students may pass. It is a cherished tradition in the community that Engine Company 46 pulls up its shiny red fire truck on Thursday mornings, weather permitting, and tests its hose, spraying water and rainbows across Spreckels Lake.

Rounding the lake, look west to see, across the continuance of Thirty-sixth Avenue, the yacht club building for the miniatures. Inside are benches on which the handsome little craft are built to specifications equally as rigid as their full-sized counterparts and a tank, or dry dock, in which to test them. Some of

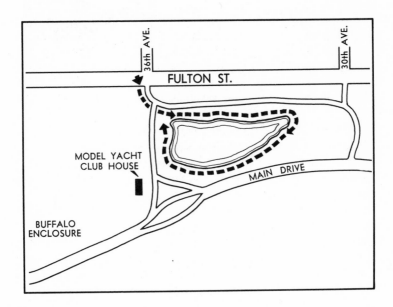

Spreckels Lake has tiny sailors and a fisherman.

the club members are devoted to sail. Others are power men. All are proud that their club, which originated in 1901, is the second oldest in the United States, topped only by Marblehead.

If you arrive at the right time, you may see a miniature fireboat in action, or a model of the battleship *Missouri* shooting blanks, or a steam job may putt noisily past. But for romance, wait for a red sunset—and sails.

40

A Walk Where
the Buffalo Roam

The Buffalo Paddock in Golden Gate Park, whose cir-
cumambulation is one of the unusual walks of San Francisco, is
in the grand tradition of royal preserves and gentlemen's estates.
It is occupied by a breeding herd of eighteen to twenty-two
placid, oxlike animals of the genus *Bison bison,* popularly
called the buffalo and far less plentiful than the nickel that once
bore its image.

To play the country squire, don your tweeds, bring a sack
of stale bread and a camera, then rally to the hunting ground to
stalk the buffalo. You will find it off John F. Kennedy Drive just
east of the Chain of Lakes and about parallel with Thirty-eighth
Avenue.

Begin this walk on John F. Kennedy Drive in the fenced
alley between the paddock and a smaller holding pen, occasionally used to separate the animals. The heavy-headed bison,
massive black shoulders thrust forward, can often be found at
the manger here, flicking their tails as they munch.

All of them are descendants from two cows named Madame Sarah Bernhardt and Princess and a bull called Ben Harrison that ranged the Montana plains until the far-sighted San Francisco Park Commission of 1890 purchased them. Originally they were installed with "two sociable emus" in a paddock handy to the grounds of the Midwinter Fair of 1894 where the buffalo were pastured until about 1924.

At that time the first paddock went to the park nursery, which was ousted from its site near Stanyan Street by construction of Kezar Stadium. At various times the herd has numbered as high as 100. Elk, bears, beavers, sheep, kangaroos, and moose also have roamed in park meadows and there was a two-acre aviary until Fleischhacker Zoo was built.

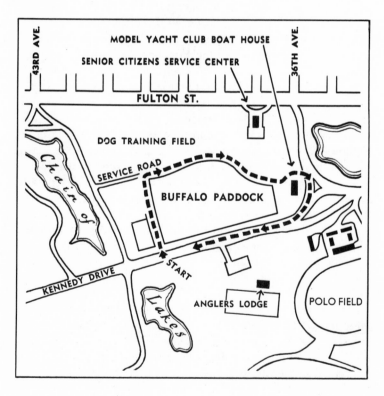

Walk north between the fences, often closed off for transfer of animals but open occasionally as a special courtesy by the staff that cares for the animals.

If you brought bread to feed the buffalo, notice that a "pecking order" prevails. The youngest calves born last winter may be nudged away from your proffered snack by older cows who in turn are ousted by bulls. None, however, is a bully of the paddock to compare with Ben Harrison II, a bull named for his sire and born to Mme. Sarah in 1894. Ben the Second often escaped and chased the mounted park police until he was gored to death by three younger bulls in 1901. His head was subsequently stuffed and presented to the M. H. de Young Memorial Museum.

If the buffalo are not at the feeding troughs, follow the fences north until you reach a service road, then bear right on it near the small dog-training circle. This will take you through a eucalyptus grove between the paddock and a larger dog-training field. Soon the gum trees are succeeded by a tremendous stand of Bishop pines and the dog field by a French *pétanque* court. At the end of the paddock, bear right again.

The Golden Gate Park Senior Citizens Center, formerly the Police Academy, will be visible through trees on your left. In front of you will be the Model Yacht Club boathouse. By bearing ever right on the path that leads in front of it, you will fully encircle the paddock.

If you have the time to spare, make a short digression behind the boathouse to see the stump where the squirrels are fed during the winter. Then end this walk where you began it on Kennedy Drive near the paddock alley where the buffalo roam.

41

A Quiet Morning Walk

"If you had to entertain Henry David Thoreau as a visiting fireman in San Francisco, where would you take him walking?" an expatriate from Boston challenged, not so long ago.

This may sound like a large order for a contemporary city to provide, but the answer is easy. One of the choicest walks in San Francisco, richly varied in its topography and vegetation, alive with raft-building boys, nest-building mallards, and other forms of wildlife, is a half-mile ramble around the Chain of Lakes near the western end of Golden Gate Park.

Thoreau, who believed some wildwood is essential to every city, if only for the enrichment of the souls of its inhabitants, would be stunned to find that three adjacent ponds could be so different, but he would feel at home here. The place to begin this adventure would be the park entrance at Forty-first Avenue and Lincoln Way. The time to take him would be in the inspiring first silver light of morning, when the day, newly washed in last night's fog, unfolds hopefully.

Once he has crossed South Drive and found the gleaming little South Lake, the walker may meet a scuttling family of quail, or a skunk out for a morning stroll.

Another roadway crosses near the Bercut Equitation Field, named for one-time Park Commissioner Peter Bercut, well-known horseman and a gardener. Walk away from it east of

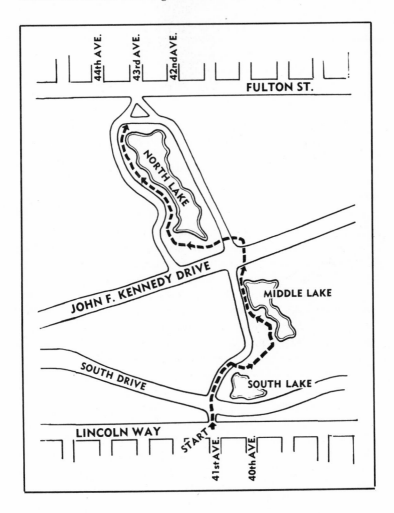

the cross-park road to find Middle Lake, which is looped by a path. One of the biggest eucalypti in the park stands between South and Middle lakes.

The perceptive walker will be aware that the character of foliage changes abruptly beyond the big tree to become predominantly Oriental. At the southern end is a stand of tule reeds, which looks like a great, unkempt mass of coarse hair, but makes fine cover for migrating waterfowl. Old Japanese cherry trees and camellias border the lake, interspersed with bamboo and pampas grass.

Cut catercorner at the intersection of John F. Kennedy Drive and the cross-park, shortcut road to find North Lake. This pond mimics the great swamps of Florida. Visitors, many of whom have been led to believe the swamp cypress, *Taxodium distichium,* exists nowhere but in the Everglades, are often startled to find the great trees up to their knobby knees in water.

A nine-hole golf course and the archery field lie west of North Lake. The Buffalo Paddock and the dog-trimmed field border the east side. Old *Leptospermum,* or "tea trees," looming out of the earth like grounded Loch Ness monsters, shield the lake shore from these successfully.

North Lake ends, usually in a great cacophony of duck conversation, near Forty-third Avenue and Fulton Street. Thoreau, tireless and a man of inquiring mind, would probably want to head back into the park to have a look at the microscopic *Radiolaria,* the oldest fossils in the Bay Area, which are to be found in the convoluted shales around Rainbow Falls, off the main drive near 20th Avenue. Walkers who don't know schist from shinola can look, instead, for the boy-made rafts along the western shore of North Lake.

42

Golf in the Park

"A golf course in Golden Gate Park!" a friend exclaimed when I mentioned it the other day. "I don't believe it!"

Like hundreds of people, she has often driven by the little-known nine-hole, "pitch 'n putt" golf course in the park and never seen it. Nevertheless it is there, sprawling generously over twenty acres of land near the northwest corner of the park, cunningly tucked behind trees and berms. A walk around its perimeter is one of the best dog walks in the park. It is also one of those restful, countrylike outings that restores the soul to a walker.

Embark on this walk at the Forty-third Avenue and Fulton Street entrance to the park. Bear west at the fork of the road that divides to go around North Lake, the northernmost of the Chain of Lakes. There in the grove of trees on the west side of the road at the first curve one will find a footpath that rambles westerly through "The Forest," as gardeners call it. Follow the path through the trees. There are golfers far off to the south, but from this forest path one is unaware of them. Dog lovers will like it because there are no picnic tables, children's play equipment, or other people attracters.

After about the distance of three and a half city blocks, the land slopes to reveal an open meadow below, usually set with upright hay bales and lively with archers. For safety, take the path as it veers north out onto Fulton Street. Then turn back into the park a few hundred feet west at Forty-seventh Avenue. Walk south past the ten-acre archery field.

Until just about twenty years ago, a U.S. Coast Guard life-saving station, manned day and night by a crew of ten, two lifeboats, a Cape Cod dory and a Lyle gun for shooting lifelines aboard distressed vessels, was situated two blocks west. Park

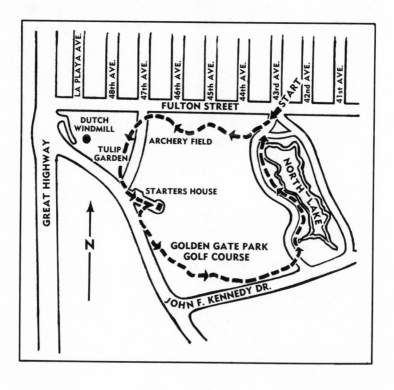

Coffee and sandwiches are for sale in the Starters House.

goers occasionally got an unexpected thrill when some large ship in distress needed assistance. Now a "moon crater" or natural dune area fills the site, concealing (but not very well) a few buildings that would be better underground.

As you walk, look west for glimpses of the North Mill. Queen Wilhelmina Tulip Garden is not visible from this path, but the circle of logs seen through the trees is sometimes used by Boy Scouts and Girl Scouts. East of the path one suddenly becomes aware of cars, parked like a strange metal intrusion. Overlooking them, a hundred feet uphill, is the starter's house for Golden Gate Park Golf Course. If you long for coffee or a sandwich, this is the ideal spot to stop. Linger awhile on a bench in the sun to see the golfers warm up.

Designed by Jack Fleming, the course was officially opened on April 4, 1951. Its clock-operated automatic sprinklers were the first in the Bay Area. Many golfers begin here, get the feel of the clubs, move on to one of the tougher city courses, Lincoln for example, then finally tackle Harding, the city's championship course. Park golf concessionaries have pooled their talents to conduct summer golf clinics for children at several courses.

When you have enjoyed the respite, return to the asphalt path that borders the road. Continue south on it, then east uphill into the trees again as John F. Kennedy Drive below rounds McLean's Bend, which takes its name from the first gardener who worked in this area of the park. From this high vantage, the walker can easily see why drivers are unaware of the golf course. He can also watch golfers on the greens. Stay on the walk for your own safety, although a thick grove of trees makes a wide buffer zone.

To make a complete loop back to Forty-third Avenue at Fulton, leave the walk that parallels Kennedy Drive at the first crossroad. Walk north along the trail that borders North Lake.

43

Ramble the Western Perimeter

Golden Gate Park now ends, for better or for worse, at Great Highway, instead of at the jade green Pacific Ocean. The strip of concrete earlier San Franciscans called The Esplanade, and the sand along the "Sundown Sea," as the native Costanoan Indians called the Pacific, is within the Golden Gate National Recreation Area. If bureaucracy doesn't compromise everything into nonentity, it's a change that could, in time, increase the public's enjoyment of these precious parts of what is coming to be known as "our urban heritage."

By whatever name, the western border of the park is unique, partly for its windmills, partly for a little known trail that links them (an old roadbed of the Park and Ocean Railroad), and partly for a few surprises along the way. It's a good walk, remarkably rural, yet surrounded by people. If you haven't explored it, take a friend or two, or your dog. Transport yourself, preferably by Muni 5 McAllister, 18 Sloat or 38 Geary to Fulton Street and La Playa. If you had come here, barely ten years ago, this area would have been Playland, the Disneyland of its day. When Mayor Adolph Sutro lived at Sutro Heights, it was the Golden Gate Ostrich Farm, supplying plumes for the big-brimmed Merry Widow hats of San Francisco's ladies of fashion.

From the south side of Fulton Street, walk to the northwest corner of the park, which is oddly bald. In 1870, when hemp was considered an innocuous agricultural crop used for burlap bags and the Coast Guard spent most of its time on sea rescue, instead of narcotics raids, this was a U. S. Coast Guard life-saving station site enclosed in a neat white picket fence. The present chain link fence makes a temporary yard, housing

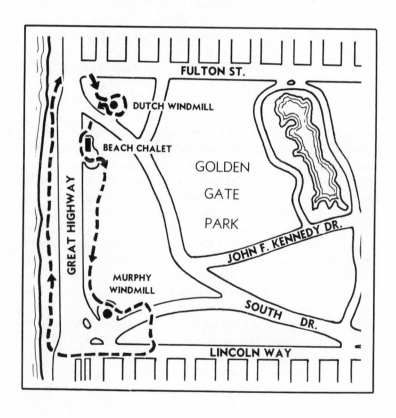

materials to repair the big Dutch, or North, Windmill looming overhead.

Follow the path through the shrubbery on your left to see renovations underway, due to the valiant efforts of Eleanor Rossi Crabtree, daughter of a former mayor, who has raised cash for supplies. Labor is donated by the Seabees and men of the U.S.S. *Coral Sea*. When first built in 1903, the cost of North Mill was $25,000. In a fresh breeze, the big sails were capable of pumping 30,000 gallons of underground water an hour to Stow Lake. Electricity puts the water into the park's irrigation system today, albeit less thriftily.

Tulips on the east side of the mill are part of the Queen Wilhelmina garden. Trees beyond hide the basin of a long-dried pond. When you have explored the environs, retrace your steps west past the windmill into the trough wide enough to accommodate a roadbed. Tracks of the Park and Ocean Railroad, like many others in the West, were torn up during World War II to make rifle barrels.

Bear south, going safely as the railroad cars once did, under Kennedy Drive. You will emerge from the underpass near the Beach Chalet. Go up the footpath to find beside the building a long concrete trough which opens to a second underpass, this one under Great Highway. Early maps show a Cyclist's Pavilion on this site, but, for contemporary San Franciscans, it was for 70 years the home of the *Gjoa*, the '69 Norwegian herring sloop Captain Roald Amundsen sailed into the Arctic to establish the position of the magnetic North Pole. After three rugged years in the Arctic, on October 19, 1906, the *Gjoa* sailed into San Francisco Bay in a howling storm, just six months after the city herself had been demolished by the great earthquake and fire. This was one of the times San Francisco earned her reputation as the City That Knows How, by honoring the crew of seven with a feast frequented by 250 celebrants at the already-restored St. Francis Hotel banquet hall (although guests were still housed at the time in the Little St. Francis in Union Square). Three years later, the *Gjoa* was towed off Ocean Beach, beached and horsed across Great Highway to this spot. Her last journey, just

Amundsen's ship, the Gjoa, before its return to Norway.

a few years ago, was back to Norway. A plaque commemorates the valiant Norsemen.

Early maps of the park also show the Beach Chalet on the ocean side of the road. It was, of course, the road that was changed, thanks to the skillful planning of M. M. O'Shaughnessy, the city engineer who created the long successful balustrade and sea wall. Originally, the wall was intended to go all the way to the Zoo, but never made it. Veterans of Foreign Wars operate a funky bar in the lower level of the Chalet, but nonmembers, who look in to see the Lucien Labaudt murals painted during the WPA years, 1936–37, are tolerated. Far-sighted citizens would like to see the upper level used for a restaurant overlooking the water.

When you have examined the Beach Chalet, return to the old roadbed behind it and continue south. If you hear shouts, climb the berm on your left to discover soccer players at practice. From October to July, the Teutonia, Mercury, Viking, Hakoah and Olympic teams compete here every Sunday.

As you walk, Murphy's Windmill, a gift from banker Samuel G. Murphy, will shortly loom up over the shrubbery like a lugubrious face looking down its nose at the Richmond-Sunset Sewage Plant (which citizens today believe could have been better sited elsewhere, or at least underground). When the arms of the mill were functioning, they were 57 feet from center to tip, made of Oregon pine, tapering from two feet thick in the middle to eight inches at the ends. Reputed to be the biggest mill in the world, it could pump 40,000 gallons an hour.

Walk past the mill to find beyond it a place where a walker can cross South Drive. It isn't easy to do at this auto-dominated end of the park. When you come out at Lincoln Way near 47th, bear right, or west, and cross Great Highway to the Beach, to make your way back to your starting point along the sand.

INDEX

169

GOLDEN G

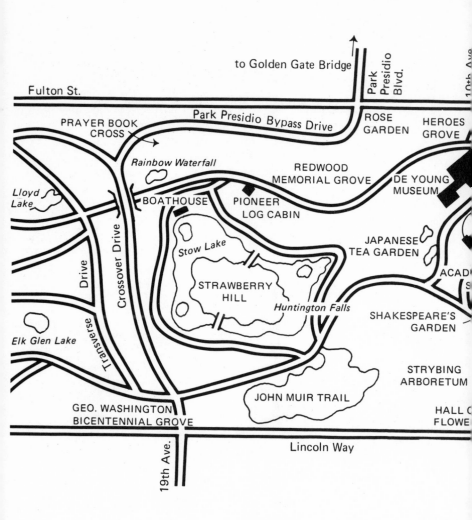

to Golden Gate Bridge

Park Presidio Blvd.

10th Ave.

Fulton St.

Park Presidio Bypass Drive

PRAYER BOOK CROSS

ROSE GARDEN

HEROES GROVE

Rainbow Waterfall

REDWOOD MEMORIAL GROVE

DE YOUNG MUSEUM

Lloyd Lake

BOATHOUSE

PIONEER LOG CABIN

JAPANESE TEA GARDEN

ACAD

Drive

Crossover Drive

Stow Lake

STRAWBERRY HILL

Huntington Falls

SHAKESPEARE'S GARDEN

Elk Glen Lake

Transverse

STRYBING ARBORETUM

JOHN MUIR TRAIL

GEO. WASHINGTON BICENTENNIAL GROVE

HALL O FLOWE

19th Ave.

Lincoln Way

AT YOU